MW01267945

Excel 2019 Formulas and Functions Study Guide

M.L. HUMPHREY

SELECT TITLES BY M.L. HUMPHREY

EXCEL ESSENTIALS 2019
Excel 2019 Beginner
Excel 2019 Intermediate
Excel 2019 Formulas & Functions

EXCEL ESSENTIALS 2019 STUDY GUIDES
Excel 2019 Formulas and Functions Study Guide

ACCESS ESSENTIALS 2019
Access 2019 Beginner
Access 2019 Intermediate

WORD ESSENTIALS 2019
Word 2019 Beginner
Word 2019 Intermediate

POWERPOINT ESSENTIALS 2019
PowerPoint 2019 Beginner
PowerPoint 2019 Intermediate

CONTENTS

CONTENTS (CONT.)

CONTENTS (CONT.)

CONTENTS (CONT.)

INTRODUCTION

This is a companion book written to complement *Excel 2019 Formulas & Functions* by M.L. Humphrey.

It is geared towards those who are already familiar with the functions covered in that book who now want to test their knowledge through quizzes. It may also be useful for those who learn better from a question and answer format.

The quizzes in this book are in the same order as in Excel 2019 Formulas & Functions but are sometimes grouped by related functions. So one quiz might cover, for example, functions related to dates.

The first section of the book just has the questions, the next section of the book has the questions as well as the answers. There is also a bonus section that contains exercises where you can test your knowledge of the various functions by applying them to specific real-life scenarios.

I encourage you to try to do each exercise first without looking at the solutions, since in the real world you'll be faced with a problem that needs solved and no one will be there to tell you which functions to use.

However, I would also encourage you to have Excel open as you work each exercise so you can use the help functions within Excel to find the functions you need. Don't feel like you need to memorize every function in Excel in order to use it effectively; you just need to know what's possible and then what keywords or phrasing to use to help you find the right function.

Alright, then. Let's start with the first quiz.

QUIZZES

HOW FORMULAS AND FUNCTIONS WORK

1. What is the difference between a formula and a function?

2. What starting symbols can you use to indicate to Excel that you are writing a formula?

3. Does a formula have to start with a function?

4. Can a formula use more than one function?

5. What are the basic components of a function?

6. If you enter a formula in Excel and then hit enter, what are you going to see in that cell in your worksheet?

7. If you want to see the actual formula that's in a cell, how can you do that?

8. If you double-click into a cell with a formula, what will Excel do to any cell references that are part of the formula?

9. How do you leave a cell that has a formula in it when you've double-clicked on the cell?

BASIC MATH CALCULATIONS

1. What are the symbols you can use for (a) adding, (b) subtracting, (c) multiplying, and (d) dividing in Excel?

2. What do the following formulas do?

$$A. =3+2$$
$$B. =3-2$$
$$C. =3*2$$
$$D. =3/2$$
$$E. =4+(3*2)$$
$$F. =4+3*2$$
$$G. =(4+3)*2$$
$$H. =2^3$$

3. What do the following formulas do?

$$A. =A1+C1$$
$$B. =A1-C1$$
$$C. =A1*C1$$

D. =A1/C1
E. =E1+(A1*C1)
F. =E1+A1*C1
G. =(E1+A1)*C1
H. =A1^B1

4. What do examples E, F, and G from the last two questions above demonstrate?

5. What's a best practice when building a really complex formula in Excel?

6. What does the phrase "garbage in, garbage out" mean with respect to Excel formulas?

WHERE TO FIND FUNCTIONS

1. Where can you go in Excel 2019 to look for a function to perform a specific task?

2. What are the categories of functions available in Excel?

3. If you bring up the Insert Function dialogue box and are looking to perform a specific task with a function, where can you search for that?

4. What happens when you click on a function name under Select a Function in the Insert Function dialogue box?

5. If that's not enough information, what can you do?

6. What happens when you select a function from the Insert Function dialogue box by clicking on it and then clicking on OK?

7. If you already know the function you want to use, but aren't sure of the inputs or the order they need to be entered in, what can you do from within a cell in your Excel worksheet?

8. If you click on the function name after you've typed, =FUNCTION_NAME(what will you get?

9. What if you still can't figure out what function to use?

FORMULA AND FUNCTION BEST PRACTICES

1. Name five best practices when working with formulas or functions.

2. Explain what it means to make your assumptions visible.

3. Explain what it means to use paste special-values when you're done with your calculations and when you should not do this.

4. How can you paste special-values to replace a formula with the result of the formula?

5. Explain why you should store your raw data in one location and work on a copy of that data instead.

6. What's another best practice when doing a lot of complex work with a dataset that requires multiple steps and manipulations?

7. What's a good naming convention to use for multiple versions of the same file?

8. Why should you test your formulas before applying them to a large data set?

9. Why can't you just accept the results Excel gives you? Why should you always "gut check" those results?

10. What does it mean to keep your audience in mind?

COPYING FORMULAS

1. What happens when you copy a formula from one cell to another?

2. If you write a formula and you want to fix the reference to a specific cell so that even if the formula is copied elsewhere it continues to reference that cell, how can you do this?

3. What if you just want to lock the row reference but not the entire cell reference?

4. What if you just want to lock the column reference but not the entire cell reference?

5. If you just want to move a formula to a new location without it changing, what's the best way to do that?

6. What does fixing cell references have to do with formulas that use a cell range, for example, a calculation

of the percent of the total for each value in Rows 1 through 25 of Column A.

TOP 10 FUNCTIONS – PART 1

1. What is the function you can use to sum a range of values or a range of cells?

2. How would you write a formula to sum the values in Column A?

3. How would you write a formula to sum the values in Rows 1 through 3?

4. How would you write a formula to sum the values in Columns A, C, and E?

5. How would you write a formula to sum the values in Cells A1 through B6?

6. How would you write a formula to subtract the total of all customer orders in Column C from the amount collected which is listed in Cell F1?

7. What functions can you use to round numbers? Which is the primary function to use? How do they differ?

8. What is the difference between using one of the rounding functions and just formatting a number to display a certain number of decimal places?

9. If you want to round the number 234.561 to the nearest whole number, how would you write that formula?

10. What if you wanted to round it to one decimal place?

11. What if you wanted to round it to two decimal places?

12. What if you wanted to round it to the nearest 100's (so 200)?

13. If I tell Excel to round a number to the nearest four decimal places, but there are only two decimal places in the number now, what will Excel do?

14. How does Excel decide with the ROUND function whether to round up or to round down?

15. What function will return a random whole number between two values you specify?

16. If I want to return any whole number between 0 and 100, how can I do that?

17. What do you need to be careful of when using the RAND or RANDBETWEEN functions?

18. How can you work around this if you need to capture that value?

19. What is the drawback to doing so?

20. What does the CONVERT function do?

21. Name three categories of conversions CONVERT can do:

22. What happens if you use units from two different categories in the same CONVERT function?

23. Are the units used in the CONVERT function case-sensitive?

24. Write the formula for converting 57 degrees Fahrenheit to Celsius:

25. Write the formula for determining how many days there are in five years using the CONVERT function:

26. Give a likely explanation for why the value returned in the last example is a decimal:

27. Write the formula for converting 60 miles to kilometers.

TOP 10 FUNCTIONS – PART 2

1. What function can you use to join text entries that are in more than one cell, such as a table of values where first name, middle name, and last name are in separate columns?

2. Write a function that joins text in Cells A2, B2, and C2 together with a space between the entries and ignoring any blank values.

3. Write a function that joins text in Cells A2, B2, and C2 together with a space between the entries but without ignoring any blank values. Explain what the result would look like if the value in Cell B2 were blank.

4. Write a function that joins text in Cells A2, B2, and C2 together with no space between the entries but without ignoring any blank values. Explain what the result would look like if the value in Cell B2 were blank.

5. What delimiter would you use if you were trying to create a list of entries separated by a comma (such as one, two, three)?

6. Can you use multiple delimiters with this function? How? Are there any challenges to doing so?

7. What function can you use to remove excess spaces from text in a cell. For example, double spaces between words or spaces before or after your text? What does this function do?

8. How would you write a formula where you wanted to combine that function with CONCATENATE(A1," ",B1," ",C1) in one cell so that excess spaces were automatically removed?

9. What do you need to be careful of when using any of the above functions? What can you do when you're done with your manipulation to address this?

10. What does the TODAY function do?

11. How do you write it?

12. Why would you use it?

13. If you wanted to calculate how many days it's been since someone purchased your product, which is the better option: have a cell that uses =TODAY() and then another cell that calculates days since purchase or just have a cell that calculates days since purchase and incorporates TODAY() into the formula? Why?

TOP 10 FUNCTIONS – PART 3

1. What are the two base functions you could use if you want to write a formula that returns one result if X is true and another if it isn't?

2. Write a formula that applies a 10% discount for any customer who buys at least $100 in merchandise assuming that the purchase amount is listed in Cell A1.

3. Explain what this formula is doing:
=IFS(B7>=B2,C2,B7>=B1,C1,TRUE,0)

4. What is one trick you can use when you get stuck building a complex formula that uses multiple if conditions?

5. What does the AND function do?

6. What is =AND(A1>5,A2>4) asking?

7. What is =AND(A1>B1,A2>B2) asking?

8. What is =IF(AND(A1="Jones",B1="Whatsit"),C1,D1) doing?

9. What does VLOOKUP do?

10. What must you do if you're using VLOOKUP on a table?

11. What's the best use for VLOOKUP?

12. Do the values in a reference table need to be an exact match for the value you're looking for when using VLOOKUP?

13. With VLOOKUP can the column that has the values you're looking up be located anywhere in your data?

14. How do you tell Excel whether to look for an exact match or an approximate match?

15. What is the difference between an exact match and an approximate match?

16. What is =VLOOKUP(25,A1:E10,3,FALSE) saying to do?

17. What is =VLOOKUP(25,A1:E10,2,TRUE) saying to do?

18. What do you need to be careful of when using VLOOKUP with apparent numbers or dates?

19. What should you always do when using any function in Excel?

THE BASE FUNCTIONS

1. Write a formula that uses a function to calculate the average of the numeric values in Cells A1 through A5.

2. How would that calculation work if one of the cells in the range where you are trying to take an average is blank?

3. What can you do to make sure that Excel includes all cells within the specified range when taking an average?

4. When using the AVERAGE function, what happens if one of the cells in your average range contains text?

5. What can you do to make sure that Excel includes cells with text in them when calculating an average over a range of cells?

6. Can you take an average of the returns of a TRUE/FALSE series of responses to get the overall percent of responses that were true? How?

7. If I have four cells with the values 2, 6, Other, and Now, what result will I get using AVERAGE? What result will I get using AVERAGEA?

8. What does the COUNT function allow you to do?

9. Does COUNT include cells with text in them?

10. Does COUNT include cells with formulas in them that create a number or date?

11. Does COUNT include cells with formulas in them that create a text entry?

12. If a cell contains "1 unit" as its value, will COUNT count it?

13. Write a formula using COUNT on a range of cells from B2 through D8.

14. What function can you use if you also want to count cells that contain text in them?

15. What does this function allow you to do?

16. What happens when you have a function in a cell, say =CONCATENATE(A1,B1,C1) but that cell is currently not displaying a value and you use each of the count functions?

17. What should you always do when using any function?

18. What does COUNTBLANK do?

19. If you have an issue with which cells are being counted by a specific count function, what should you do?

20. If you want the minimum value within a range, what function can you use to get it?

21. If you want the maximum value within a range, what function can you use to get it?

22. How would you write the formula to calculate the minimum value in Column D?

23. How would you write the formula to calculate the maximum value in Row 3?

24. What value will Excel return if you ask for the minimum or maximum of a range of values that have no numbers in them?

25. What will happen if you try to take the minimum or maximum of a range of values that has an error value in it such as #DIV/0!?

26. If you have a range of values that you want to take a minimum of but that range includes TRUE and FALSE entries that you want included in the calculation, what function should you use?

27. How do MINA and MAXA treat TRUE or FALSE values?

28. How do MINA and MAXA treat text?

29. What result will you get from =MINA(A1:A3) where A1 is the word Other, A2 is 2, and A3 is 3? What about =MIN(A1:A3)?

30. What result will you get from =MINA(A1:A3) where A1 is -2, A2 is 2, and A3 is 3? What about =MIN(A1:A3)?

31. What result will you get from =MAXA(A1:A3) where A1 is -2, A2 is 2, and A3 is 3? What about =MAX(A1:A3)?

32. What result will you get from =MAXA(A1:A3) where A1 is -2, A2 is 2, and A3 is Title? What about =MAX(A1:A3)?

THE LOGICAL* FUNCTIONS

1. What does the OR function do?

2. What is =OR(A1>5,A2>4) asking?

3. What is =IF(OR(A1="Canton",B1="Toledo"),G1, G1*2) doing?

4. What do the TRUE and FALSE functions do?

5. When might you use them?

6. What does the NA function do?

7. When might you use the NA function?

8. What do you need to remember when using the TRUE, FALSE, or NA functions?

9. What functions is the NOT function related to?

10. Why do I encourage you to find a way to use a function other than the NOT function to build a formula?

11. What result will you get if you use =NOT(FALSE)?

THE IF FUNCTIONS

1. What do you need to be aware of when using the various IF functions if someone with an older version of Excel might use your worksheet?

2. What function would you use if you had a table of sales data and wanted to know the average transaction amount for customers in Montana who bought Whatsits?

3. Write a formula that takes the average of the values in Column C when the values in Column A are "MT" and the values in Column B are "Whatsits" and the data to be used is in Rows 1 through 6.

4. What function would you use if you had a table of sales data and wanted to know the number of transaction where customers in Montana bought Whatsits?

5. Write a formula that counts the number of results where the value in Column A is "MT" and the value in

Column B is "Whatsits" and the data to be used is in
Rows 1 through 6.

6. What function would you use if you had a table of
sales data and wanted to know sum the amount that
customers in Montana who bought Whatsits have spent?

7. Write a formula that sum the amount that customers
spent which listed in Column C when the values in
Column A are "MT" and the values in Column B are
"Whatsits" and the data to be used is in Rows 1 through
6.

8. What function would you use if you had a table of
sales data and wanted to know the minimum amount any
customer from Montana who bought Whatsits spent?
What function would you use if you wanted to know the
maximum amount spent.

9. Write a formula that finds the minimum amount spent
when transaction amount is in Column C for cases where
the value in Column A was "MT" and the value in
Column B was "Whatsits" and the data to be used is in
Rows 1 through 6.

10. What is one way to troubleshoot a complex IF or IFS
function that involves multiple conditions?

11. With an IF function that has multiple conditions,
what should you always check for?

12. Use IF to write a formula that looks at the value in
Cell A1 and if it is greater than 10 returns a result of A,

if it is greater than 5 and up to a value of 10 returns a result of B, and if it is 5 or less returns a value of C. Write the same formula using IFS.

13. If you want to count how many times the values in Cells C10 through C25 are greater than the value in Cell A1, how would you write that?

14. What do you need to watch out for when using COUNTIFS, SUMIFS, AVERAGEIFS, MINIFS, and MAXIFS?

15. What do the asterisk (*), the question mark (?), and the tilde (~) represent when you're writing a count, sum, average, min, or max criteria?

16. With COUNTIFS, SUMIFS, AVERAGEIFS, MINIFS, and MAXIFS if you have three criteria you specify and two of the three are met, what will happen with that entry?

17. Why is this important?

18. What function can you use to suppress an #N/A! result in a formula?

19. Apply that function to the following formula: =VLOOKUP(D:D,'Advertising Spend By Series'!E:F,2,FALSE) so that a value of 0 is returned instead of the #N/A! error message.

20. Now apply the function to the following formula: =VLOOKUP(D:D,'Advertising Spend By Series'!E:F,2,

FALSE)so that a value of "No Match" is returned instead of the #N/A! error message.

21. And also apply the function to the following formula: =VLOOKUP(D:D,'Advertising Spend By Series'!E:F,2, FALSE) so that a blank value is returned instead of the #N/A! error message.

22. What function can you use to suppress all error messages instead of just #N/A!?

23. Apply that function to a situation where you are dividing the value in Cell A1 by the value in Cell B1 and you want to return a blank result instead of an error message.

24. Now apply that function to a situation where you are dividing the value in Cell A1 by the value in Cell B1 and you want to return a value of "Error" instead of a specific error message.

25. What is the danger in using IFNA or IFERROR?

26. What is one way of addressing this issue?

THE LOOKUP FUNCTIONS – PART 1

1. What does the HLOOKUP function do?

2. What will this formula do: =HLOOKUP("April", B1:M12,4,FALSE)

3. What can you look up using HLOOKUP?

4. If you look up a text string, what do you need to be sure to do?

5. What are wildcards and how can you use them when looking up text?

6. In the table you're going to search using HLOOKUP, where do the values you're searching for need to be?

7. In the table you're going to search using HLOOKUP, where do the values you want to return need to be?

8. What is the difference between using FALSE and TRUE as the final criteria for the HLOOKUP function?

9. What is the risk to using TRUE as the third input to the HLOOKUP function?

10. Can you sort the values in a row in ascending order?

11. When you tell Excel which row to pull your result from using HLOOKUP, what number do you need to provide? Is it the Row number in the worksheet or something else?

12. If you provide a row value of 1 in the HLOOKUP function what will that return, assuming there is a result to return?

13. If you ask HLOOKUP to find an exact match and there isn't one, what value will Excel return?

14. What could potentially result in an incorrect error message when using HLOOKUP?

15. What does the SWITCH function do?

16. Write a formula using the SWITCH function that tells someone they are correct if the value in Cell A1 is 50 and incorrect if it's any other value.

17. Write a formula using the SWITCH function that assigns all Grade 9 students to A Rotation, all Grade 10 students to B Rotation, all Grade 11 students to C Rotation, and all Grade 12 students to D Rotation,

assuming that Cell A1 contains the grade number. Include a condition for when a student is not listed with a grade or listed with a grade other than 9, 10, 11, or 12.

18. If you were using the SWITCH function and anticipated that your assignments (such as A Rotation, etc.) were going to change over time, what is one way to build the formula so that it was easier to modify it later?

19. What does the CHOOSE function do?

20. When is CHOOSE most powerful?

21. What will the result be of =CHOOSE(3,1,2,3) be? Why?

THE LOOKUP FUNCTIONS – PART 2

1. What does the TRANSPOSE function do?

2. Does TRANSPOSE work on a table of values that covers multiple rows and/or columns?

3. What do you have to do special because TRANSPOSE is an array formula?

4. If you want to take the values in Cells C1 through C5 and place them in Cells E8 through I8, how would you do that?

5. If all you want to do is change the orientation of your data but not keep a reference to the original cells, what is a better option?

6. What is the difference between using the TRANSPOSE function and using Paste-Transpose?

7. What are the two tasks that the INDEX function can perform?

8. What is the following formula supposed to do:
=INDEX(A2:E7,3,4)

9. Does the INDEX function require you to include a header row or row labels in the specified cell range?

10. How do you determine the row number value to use in the INDEX function?

11. How do you determine the column number value to use in the INDEX function?

12. Can you use the INDEX function with more than one table of data? How?

13. What happens if you use the fourth variable in the INDEX function without providing multiple table range values in the first variable?

14. If you want to use the INDEX function to pull an entire column or row of data, what do you need to do?

15. Can you easily copy and paste an array formula?

16. Once you've extracted values from a table using the INDEX function are the results fixed values?

17. What does the MATCH function do?

18. If the MATCH function returns a value of 2 for the following formula, what does that mean:
=MATCH($A12,$A$2:$A$7,0)

19. What is the value in using the MATCH function?

20. What kinds of values can MATCH look for?

21. What are the three match types that you can use with MATCH?

22. If you're not looking for an exact match what do you need to do first? And how will your choice of match type impact this?

23. What is the default match type used by MATCH? Why is this a problem?

24. Is the value returned by MATCH the row number or the column number in the worksheet or something else?

THE STATISTICAL FUNCTIONS

1. What is the difference between an average, a mean, and a mode?

2. What's a good idea when dealing with a large range of data points that will help you figure out whether average, mean, or mode works best for your data?

3. How would you write the function to calculate the median of a range of values from Cells C1 through C9?

4. How does Excel calculate the median when there is an even number of values in the range?

5. Why can this be dangerous?

6. What function should you use to find the most common result when your data has a large bump or bumps that aren't near the midline?

7. How would you write this function for a range of values in Cells B2 through B10 where you just have one bump in the data?

8. What is special about the MODE.MULT function?

9. How do you use MODE.MULT?

10. If you've properly used MODE.MULT, what will it look like in the formula bar when you click back into the cell for the function?

11. If you have multi-modal data where two values occur with the same high frequency but you use the MODE.SNGL or MODE function instead of the MODE.MULT function, what will happen?

12. What can you do if you want your MODE.MULT results to display in a row instead of in a column?

13. What is one issue with MODE.MULT that you're still going to run into?

14. How could you work around this issue?

15. What function or functions can you use if you want to know the rank of a specific value within a range of possible values? In other words, is this the 5th largest number, the 10th, the 20th, etc. compared to other numbers in the range?

16. If you want to know the rank of a value in Cell A1 from within the range of Cells A1 through A15, how can

you write that function using ascending values? What about descending values?

17. To use one of the ranking functions does your data have to be sorted?

18. How do RANK.EQ and RANK.AVG differ?

19. What does the SMALL function do?

20. What does the LARGE function do?

21. Can you technically use SMALL to return the largest value in a range and LARGE to return the smallest value in a range?

22. What does the FORECAST.LINEAR function do?

23. Why is it important to remember that it only works with a linear trend?

24. Because of this, what should you do before using the FORECAST function?

25. What are the order of the inputs to the FORECAST.LINEAR function?

26. Does your data need to be sorted to use FORECAST.LINEAR?

27. What does the FREQUENCY function do?

28. What must you have in order to use the FREQUENCY function?

29. What does it mean that FREQUENCY is an array function?

30. What are the inputs to the FREQUENCY function?

31. How is a bins array entry structured? And how is it used by Excel?

32. What is an easy way to get a list of bin array values that correspond to all potential values in your data set?

33. If the range of values you want to evaluate are in Column C and your bins values are in Cells D2 through D6, how would you write the formula to calculate your frequencies for each of those bin values?

MORE MATH FUNCTIONS

1. If you had a table of data that contained customer in Column A, units bought by that customer in Column B, and price per unit in Column C and wanted to get a total spent for all customers using one function, what function could you use? How would you write it.

2. When using this function, what does the #VALUE! error message likely indicate?

3. What does Excel do with text entries included in the cell range for that function?

4. What function would you use to take the absolute value of a number?

5. Write a formula to take the absolute value of -3:

6. What function can be used to raise a number to a power? For example, to take the number 3 to the 2nd power. Write that formula.

7. Is there a way to do this without a function? How?

8. Can you use both of these methods to take a root power, such as the square root of a number? If so, write how to take the square root of 9.

9. Is there a function that will specifically let you take the square root of a number? What is it? Apply it to 9.

10. How can you derive the value of *e* using a function?

11. What is the function that will let you return the value of Pi to fifteen digits? How would you write it?

12. What is =LOG(100) asking?

13. Write a formula that uses the LOG function to determine what power you'd have to take the number 2 to in order to get a result of 24:

14. Write a formula that uses the LOG function to determine what power you'd have to take *e* to in order to get a result of 24:

15. Write a formula that uses the LN function to make the same determination:

16. What formula would you write to determine the number of possible permutations for a group of ten people?

17. What happens with the FACT function if you input a decimal value, for example =FACT(3.95)?

18. What happens if you ask for the factorial of a negative number?

19. What function would you use if you wanted to calculate the number of three-person teams that could be built out of a population of nine people. How would you write that?

20. What function would you use to determine the total number of possible outcomes for a group of nine people where you were assigning three prizes and each person in the group was allowed to win each prize even if they'd already won? How would you write that?

THE TEXT FUNCTIONS

1. If you want to convert a text string into uppercase letters, which function should you use?

2. What if you want to convert a text string into lowercase letters?

3. What if you want the initial letter of each word to be capitalized, but the rest to be in lowercase?

4. Let's say that you have a text string in Cell C10 and another in Cell C11 and that you want to combine those entries with a space between them and convert them into uppercase letters. How could you do that?

5. What does the LEFT function do? What does the RIGHT function do?

6. If you want to return the first five characters of the text in Cell A1, how would you do that?

7. Do these functions work with numbers as well?

8. What happens if the number of characters you specify is greater than the number of characters in the string you reference?

9. What happens if you don't specify a number of characters to return?

10. What does the MID function do?

11. What happens if the start point you provide for the MID function is greater than the number of characters in the string?

12. What happens if you use MID and ask Excel to return more characters than there are in the text string?

13. What other function could you use to get the same result as =MID(A1,1,2)?

14. What does Excel say that the TEXT function can do?

15. What else can the TEXT function actually do?

16. If you have a date in Cell A1 and want to pull the full name of the day of the week, how would you do that using the TEXT function?

17. What about the month of the year?

18. What does the LEN function do?

19. What result would LEN return for =LEN("This one")? Why?

20. How does LEN handle a formula in a cell?

21. What is the following formula doing:
=LEFT(A1,LEN(A1)-LEN(" units"))?

22. What does the EXACT function do?

23. Is EXACT case-sensitive?

THE DATE & TIME FUNCTIONS

1. When converted to a date what does the number 1 represent in Excel?

2. Can Excel handle dates prior to that date?

3. Can you use addition and subtraction with dates in Excel? Why or why not?

4. If you enter a two-digit year, for example '29, how will Excel treat that in terms of the century it applies?

5. What does the DATE function do?

6. What happens if you use the DATE function with a date prior to January 1, 1900, so for example if you use =DATE(1880,1,1)?

7. Can you use a value for the month portion of the DATE function that is greater than 12? What about less than 1?

8. What about days of the month? Can you have a number greater than 31 or a negative number?

9. Write a formula that takes a date stored in Cell B2 and adds four months to it.

10. What does the YEAR function do?

11. How would you use YEAR to extract the year portion of the date March 1, 2010?

12. What happens if you fail to use quotation marks around a date used in a YEAR function?

13. What are the equivalent functions to year for month, day of the month, hour, minute of the day, and seconds? What kind of value will be returned for the hour?

14. What does the WEEKDAY function do?

15. What is the default setting for the WEEKDAY function in terms of numbering the days of the week?

16. If August 13, 2019 is a Tuesday and I use =WEEKDAY("August 13, 2019") what value will I get back?

17. What portion of the WEEKDAY function should you change if you want the numbers returned to map to

different days of the week? How would you change the above formula so that Monday is treated as a 1 and Tuesday returns a value of 2 instead?

18. What does the WEEKNUM function do? What is the highest value it will return?

19. How does Excel define a week for purposes of the WEEKNUM function?

20. How do you get Excel to define a week in accordance with ISO standards when using the WEEKNUM function? And how does it work?

21. What is another function you can use to get Excel to apply the ISO standard when determining the week number?

22. What does the EDATE function do?

23. What is another way to get this same result?

24. If I use =EDATE("March 1, 2019",4) what result will that give me?

25. How does EDATE handle partial month values, such as =EDATE("March 1, 2019",4.9)?

26. What does the EOMONTH function do?

27. What does the NETWORKDAYS.INTL function do?

28. Explain what the weekend input to the NETWORKDAYS.INTL function does.

29. What does the WORKDAY.INTL function do? Is it directly interchangeable with NETWORKDAYS.INTL?

WHEN THINGS GO WRONG

1. Name five different error messages you might see.

2. What does #REF! generally indicate?

3. How can you see where the cell that was deleted was located in your formula?

4. What does a #VALUE! message indicate?

5. What does a #DIV/0! message indicate?

6. What does a #N/A error message generally mean?

7. What can you check for if this happens and you don't think it should have?

8. What does the IFERROR function do? What do you need to be careful with if you use it?

9. What does the #NUM! error message generally indicate?

10. What is a circular reference?

11. If you don't think you have a circular reference but Excel tells you you do, what should you check for?

12. If you're trying to figure out what cells are feeding the value in a cell where can you go to do that?

13. If Excel tells you you have too few arguments, what should you check for?

14. What can you do with a formula that just isn't working the way it should be?

CELL NOTATION

1. What is Cell A1 referencing?

2. Name two ways you can reference more than one cell in a function.

3. Can you reference a cell in another worksheet?

4. Can you reference a cell in another workbook?

5. What's an easy way to reference a cell in another worksheet or workbook?

QUIZ ANSWERS

HOW FORMULAS AND FUNCTIONS WORK

1. What is the difference between a formula and a function?

A formula is a way of performing a calculation or task using Excel. It can involve functions but does not have to.

A function is a command that is used as part of a formula that tells Excel to perform a pre-defined task or set of tasks. Those tasks can be mathematical (like SUM) or they can be related to text (like LEFT), dates (like YEAR), logic (like AND), and more.

2. What starting symbols can you use to indicate to Excel that you are writing a formula?

You can use a plus sign (+), a minus sign (-), or an equals sign (=). It's generally best to use an equals sign

3. Does a formula have to start with a function?

No. A formula such as =A1+SUM(B1:B5) is perfectly valid.

4. Can a formula use more than one function?
Yes.

5. What are the basic components of a function?
The function name, an opening paren, the information Excel requires to perform the function, and then a closing paren.

6. If you enter a formula in Excel and then hit enter, what are you going to see in that cell in your worksheet?
The result of the formula. So, for example, if you type =2+2 into a cell and hit enter you will see 4, the result of adding two plus two, in the cell where you entered the formula.

7. If you want to see the actual formula that's in a cell, how can you do that?
Click on the cell and look in the formula bar or double-click on the cell to see the formula in the cell itself.

8. If you double-click into a cell with a formula, what will Excel do to any cell references that are part of the formula?
It will color-code each cell reference in the formula and highlight those cells in the worksheet in the same color.

9. How do you leave a cell that has a formula in it when you've double-clicked on the cell?
Use Esc, Enter, tab, or click away. Do not use the arrow keys.

BASIC MATH CALCULATIONS

1. What are the symbols you can use for (a) adding, (b) subtracting, (c) multiplying, and (d) dividing in Excel?

    (a) To add you can use the plus sign (+)

    (b) To subtract you can use the minus sign (-)

    (c) To multiply you can use the asterisk (*)

    (d) To divide you can use the forward slash (/)

2. What do the following formulas do?

A. =3+2

    Adds 3 to 2

B. =3-2

    Subtracts 2 from 3

C. =3*2

    Multiplies 3 by 2

D. =3/2

Divides 3 by 2

E. =4+(3*2)

Multiplies 3 by 2 and then adds the result to 4

F. =4+3*2

Multiplies 3 by 2 and adds the result to 4

G. =(4+3)*2

Adds 4 to 3 and multiplies the result times 2

H. =2^3

Takes the value 2 to the 3rd power

3. What do the following formulas do?

A. =A1+C1

Adds the value in Cell A1 to the value in Cell C1

B. =A1-C1

Subtracts the value in Cell C1 from the value in Cell A1

C. =A1*C1

Multiplies the value in Cell A1 by the value in Cell C1

D. =A1/C1

Divides the value in Cell A1 by the value in Cell C1

E. =E1+(A1*C1)

Multiplies the value in Cell A1 by the value in Cell C1 and then adds the result to the value in Cell E1

F. =E1+A1*C1

Multiplies the value in Cell A1 by the value in Cell C1 and then adds the result to the value in Cell E1

G. =(E1+A1)*C1

Adds the values in Cells E1 and A1 and then multiplies them by the value in Cell C1

H. =A1^B1

Takes the value in Cell A1 to the power indicated by the value in Cell B1

4. What do examples E, F, and G from the last two questions above demonstrate?

How important it is when writing a complex formula that you place your parens in the right place, because that will determine the order in which Excel performs its calculations and will impact your answer. It also demonstrates the precedence of which calculations in Excel are performed first.

5. What's a best practice when building a really complex formula in Excel?

Build it in pieces and test that each piece is calculating correctly before combining all of the pieces together. Also, check if there's a function that would do the same calculation for you.

6. What does the phrase "garbage in, garbage out" mean with respect to Excel formulas?

It means that Excel is just a computer program. It is only as good at calculating values as the user is at giving it the right information. So if you provide the wrong inputs or write the formula wrong, Excel will not perform the calculation you want. It is up to you, the user, to provide Excel with the right information, all of the information it needs, and to present that information in the correct order and format.

WHERE TO FIND FUNCTIONS

1. Where can you go in Excel 2019 to look for a function to perform a specific task?

The Formulas tab will show you a Function Library set of dropdowns arranged by type (Financial, Logical, Text, etc.). You can hold your mouse over each one for a brief description of what it does.

If you don't know the function you want, it's better to go to Insert Function and bring up the Insert Function dialogue box. This will let you search using a few keywords for the function you want.

2. What are the categories of functions available in Excel?

Financial, Logical, Text, Date & Time, Lookup & Reference, Math & Trig, Statistical, Engineering, Cube, Information, Compatibility, Web

3. If you bring up the Insert Function dialogue box and are looking to perform a specific task with a function, where can you search for that?

In the "Search For a Function" box at the top. Enter a few keywords related to what you want to do and then click on Go. Excel will list functions in the Select a Function box that meet those keywords.

4. What happens when you click on a function name under Select a Function in the Insert Function dialogue box?

Excel will show you a brief description of what the function does as well as a sample of what inputs the function requires to work.

5. If that's not enough information, what can you do?

Click on "Help On This Function" in the bottom left corner of the dialogue box. (You could also look the function up in the Help tab.)

6. What happens when you select a function from the Insert Function dialogue box by clicking on it and then clicking on OK?

It brings up the Function Arguments dialogue box which will show you the description for the function, a sample output for the function based upon the choices you make, and input boxes for you to add the information required for the function.

7. If you already know the function you want to use, but aren't sure of the inputs or the order they need to be entered in, what can you do from within a cell in your Excel worksheet?

Type
=FUNCTION_NAME

to see the Excel description of what the function does. For example,
=IFS

Type
=FUNCTION_NAME(

to see a list of the inputs for the function and the order in which they need to appear. For example,

=IFS(

8. If you click on the function name after you've typed, =FUNCTION_NAME(what will you get?

An Excel Help task pane for that function.

9. What if you still can't figure out what function to use?

Do an internet search. Chances are someone else at some point wanted to do the exact same thing you do.

FORMULA AND FUNCTION BEST PRACTICES

1. Name five best practices when working with formulas or functions.

Make your assumptions visible, use paste special-values when you're done with your calculations, store your raw data in one location and work on a copy of that data for any calculations or manipulations of the data, test your formulas to make sure they work under all possible circumstances especially threshold cases, and consider your audience.

2. Explain what it means to make your assumptions visible.

While it's possible to write a formula that has all of the information written within a cell, it's better to show on your worksheet any inputs into that formula. For example, if I assume that selling my house is going to cost me 3% in realty fees, it's better to have a separate field in Excel that shows the assumed realty fees rather than hide that value in a formula.

3. Explain what it means to use paste special-values when you're done with your calculations and when you should not do this.

Do not do this if you expect to update your information that's feeding the calculation. This should only be done when you are completely finished with your analysis. Because if you do it and then update an input into the formula, the formula no longer exists and your final answer will not update with the new information.

If you've finished your calculation using paste special-values will lock in your results so that they can't be impacted by deleting data in the worksheet that was used to make the calculation.

4. How can you paste special-values to replace a formula with the result of the formula?

Click on the cell(s) with the formula(s), Copy (Ctrl +C), right-click on the same cell, and choose the Paste Special - Values option from the dropdown menu. (It's the one with the 123 on the clipboard.) Hit Enter or Esc.

You can also use the menu options in the Home tab to copy and paste.

5. Explain why you should store your raw data in one location and work on a copy of that data instead.

Because some things can't be undone.

For example, if you sort only part of your data and don't realize it until later your entire dataset will be useless. Or if you find and replace the wrong information. Or you remove duplicates improperly. Or you delete records.

6. What's another best practice when doing a lot of complex work with a dataset that requires multiple steps and manipulations?

Save versions of your calculations as you go after each significant manipulation is completed. This way if you do mess up at some point along the way you can go back to one of those earlier versions rather than having to start over from scratch.

7. What's a good naming convention to use for multiple versions of the same file?

One option is to use version numbers, so File V1, File V2.

Another option is to use a YYYYMMDD format. So File 20100102 and File 20100203.

8. Why should you test your formulas before applying them to a large data set?

To make sure they're working properly, especially at the thresholds.

For example, if you're using an IF function that returns one value when the value in Column A is over 25 and another value when it's under, you should test what happens when the value in Column A is equal to 25. Is that the result you want? If not, you need to edit the formula.

It's easier to catch these things in test scenarios that are designed to test the edges than in a thousand rows of data.

9. Why can't you just accept the results Excel gives you? Why should you always "gut check" those results?

Because Excel just does what you tell it to do and if you tell it to do the wrong thing it's going to do it without question. So you should always be asking yourself, "does this result make sense?" If it doesn't, you need to look at the numbers and your result to see if there's an error in your formula.

10. What does it mean to keep your audience in mind?

You should always know who the ultimate user of your Excel worksheet will be if it isn't going to be you and you should use functions that are appropriate for that user. For example, IFS is a new function in Excel 2019, so if your end user only had access to earlier versions of Excel then you wouldn't want to use IFS in that worksheet because it wouldn't work for them.

For some users of Excel a .xlsx file type also will not work for them.

And for other users the number of available rows in their version of Excel may differ from the number of available rows in your version of Excel.

COPYING FORMULAS

1. What happens when you copy a formula from one cell to another?

All cell references in the formula will adjust based upon the number of rows and columns you moved the formula. So if a formula references Cell A1 and you move it over two columns, that reference to Cell A1 will become a reference to Cell C1. And if you move it down two rows, that reference to Cell A1 will become a reference to Cell A3.

2. If you write a formula and you want to fix the reference to a specific cell so that even if the formula is copied elsewhere it continues to reference that cell, how can you do this?

By using $ signs in front of both the column and row reference. So if you use $A$1 in a formula and copy that formula, the formula will continue to reference Cell A1 no matter where you copy it to.

3. What if you just want to lock the row reference but not the entire cell reference?

Then just put a $ sign in front of the row portion of the cell reference. So, for example, A$1.

4. What if you just want to lock the column reference but not the entire cell reference?

Then just put a $ sign in front of the column portion of the cell reference. So, for example, $A1.

5. If you just want to move a formula to a new location without it changing, what's the best way to do that?

Use Cut instead of Copy. That will move the formula without changing the cell references.

6. What does fixing cell references have to do with formulas that use a cell range, for example, a calculation of the percent of the total for each value in Rows 1 through 25 of Column A.

If the calculation is percent of the total for each value in Rows 1 through 25 in Column A, you would write the first calculation as =A1/SUM(A1:A25). But to use that formula for the values in Cells A2 through A25 you'd need to fix the cell references for the range of cells used in the SUM portion of the formula. So you'd write that as =A1/SUM($A$1:$A$25) before you copied the formula down to the other rows so that the calculation was always using the values in Cells A1 through A25.

If the values in that cell range were not fixed first by using the $ signs, then the formula in each row would use a different cell range for its calculation.

TOP 10 FUNCTIONS – PART 1

1. What is the function you can use to sum a range of values or a range of cells?
   SUM

2. How would you write a formula to sum the values in Column A?
   =SUM(A:A)

3. How would you write a formula to sum the values in Rows 1 through 3?
   =SUM(1:3)

4. How would you write a formula to sum the values in Columns A, C, and E?
   =SUM(A:A,C:C,E:E)

5. How would you write a formula to sum the values in Cells A1 through B6?
   =SUM(A1:B6)

6. How would you write a formula to subtract the total of all customer orders in Column C from the amount collected which is listed in Cell F1?

=F1-SUM(C:C)

7. What functions can you use to round numbers? Which is the primary function to use? How do they differ?

ROUND, ROUNDUP, and ROUNDDOWN.

ROUND is the primary one. It will round a number either up or down depending on the value of the next digit. ROUNDUP and ROUNDDOWN will always either round away from zero or towards zero, respectively.

8. What is the difference between using one of the rounding functions and just formatting a number to display a certain number of decimal places?

Formatting the number doesn't change the underlying value of that number. So 1.234 will still be 1.234 even if it looks like it's now just 1. Whereas applying ROUND to that number will change it into the number 1 and will remove the decimal places as if they never existed.

9. If you want to round the number 234.561 to the nearest whole number, how would you write that formula?

=ROUND(234.561,0)

10. What if you wanted to round it to one decimal place?

=ROUND(234.561,1)

11. What if you wanted to round it to two decimal places?

=ROUND(234.561,2)

12. What if you wanted to round it to the nearest 100's (so 200)?

=ROUND(234.561,-2)

13. If I tell Excel to round a number to the nearest four decimal places, but there are only two decimal places in the number now, what will Excel do?

It'll leave the number as it is. =ROUND(2.34, 4) will return a value of 2.34.

14. How does Excel decide with the ROUND function whether to round up or to round down?

It looks at the digit one past where you told it to round and uses that to decide whether to round up or down. So if you have 1.2646 and tell Excel to round to two digits it will round down to 1.26 because of the 4 in the third position. It will not round up from the 6 to make the 4 a 5 and then round up from that. Digits from 0 through 4 round down. Digits from 5 through 9 round up.

15. What function will return a random whole number between two values you specify?

RANDBETWEEN

16. If I want to return any whole number between 0 and 100, how can I do that?

=RANDBETWEEN(0,100)

=INT(RAND()*100) would also work

17. What do you need to be careful of when using the RAND or RANDBETWEEN functions?

They will generate a new random value every time you recalculate your worksheet with F9, every time you do another calculation in your worksheet, and every time you open the worksheet. Once that happens, you won't be able to go back to the previously-generated random value.

18. How can you work around this if you need to capture that value?

One way is to generate your random value and then immediately use copy and paste special-values to convert the entry to a value instead of keep it as a function. Another option is to click into the cell with your formula in it, highlight that portion of the formula, hit F9, and then hit Enter to lock in the calculation as of that moment in time. You can also build a process to immediately use and lock-in that value.

19. What is the drawback to doing so?

Both of the first two approaches convert a formula to a fixed value so can only be used that one time unless you paste special-values into a different cell.

20. What does the CONVERT function do?

It converts a number from one measurement system to another.

21. Name three categories of conversions CONVERT can do:

Answers can include: Temperatures, distances, weights, units of time, units of energy, fluid measurements, speeds, etc.

22. What happens if you use units from two different categories in the same CONVERT function?

You'll receive an #N/A! error result.

23. Are the units used in the CONVERT function case-sensitive?

Yes. For example, "day" is a valid unit entry, but "Day" is not.

24. Write the formula for converting 57 degrees Fahrenheit to Celsius:

=CONVERT(57,"F","C")

25. Write the formula for determining how many days there are in five years using the CONVERT function:

=CONVERT(5,"yr","day")

26. Give a likely explanation for why the value returned in the last example is a decimal:

Because of leap years. There is one leap year every fourth year, so the calculation involves one-quarter of a day extra per year to account for that.

27. Write the formula for converting 60 miles to kilometers:

=CONVERT(60,"mi","km")

TOP 10 FUNCTIONS – PART 2

1. What function can you use to join text entries that are in more than one cell, such as a table of values where first name, middle name, and last name are in separate columns?

TEXTJOIN

Although in previous versions of Excel you could have also used CONCAT or CONCATENATE.

2. Write a function that joins text in Cells A2, B2, and C2 together with a space between the entries and ignoring any blank values.

Using TEXTJOIN, this can be written two different ways:

=TEXTJOIN(" ",TRUE,A2:C2)
=TEXTJOIN(" ",1,A2:C2)

3. Write a function that joins text in Cells A2, B2, and C2 together with a space between the entries but without ignoring any blank values.

Explain what the result would look like if the value in Cell B2 were blank.

Using TEXTJOIN, this can be written two different ways:

=TEXTJOIN(" ",FALSE,A2:C2)
=TEXTJOIN(" ",0,A2:C2)

If Cell B2 was blank then there would be two spaces between the values from Cells A2 and C2 because of the delimiter.

4. Write a function that joins text in Cells A2, B2, and C2 together with no space between the entries but without ignoring any blank values. Explain what the result would look like if the value in Cell B2 were blank.

Using TEXTJOIN, this can be written two different ways:

=TEXTJOIN("",FALSE,A2:C2)
=TEXTJOIN("",0,A2:C2)

If the value in Cell B2 is blank then the result will just be the value in A2 followed immediately by the value in C2.

5. What delimiter would you use if you were trying to create a list of entries separated by a comma (such as one, two, three)?

You could use ", "

6. Can you use multiple delimiters with this function? How? Are there any challenges to doing so?

Yes. You can do so by putting the delimiters in cells and then referencing that cell range in the delimiter field. Or you can use { } brackets to list more than one delimiter in the first input field.

One issue comes up when there are any blank cells for certain entries in your range but not others because the delimiters will be used in the wrong order for those entries with the blank cells. That's because when you list more than one delimiter, Excel is just working its way down the list of delimiters you provide each time it needs one.

The other issue comes up when you don't provide enough delimiters. In that case, Excel will start back at the top of the list.

7. What function can you use to remove excess spaces from text in a cell. For example, double spaces between words or spaces before or after your text? What does this function do?

TRIM. It removes all spaces from a text string except for single spaces between words.

8. How would you write a formula where you wanted to combine that function with CONCATENATE(A1," ",B1," ",C1) in one cell so that excess spaces were automatically removed?

=TRIM(CONCATENATE(A1," ",B1," ",C1))

9. What do you need to be careful of when using any of the above functions? What can you do when you're done with your manipulation to address this?

Your entries will look like text but they are in fact still formulas, meaning that if you change the values in the input cells (by, for example, deleting them) you will change the result of your formula. This is why it's a good idea once you're done with manipulating your text strings to copy and paste special-values to lock in the result as a text entry and remove the formulas. (But only do that when you're done and don't expect the inputs to change further.)

10. What does the TODAY function do?
Returns the current date formatted as a date.

11. How do you write it?
=TODAY() or =TODAY( )

12. Why would you use it?
It can be used as part of a calculation that's looking at how many days from today something needs to happen or did happen. For example, days past due on a payment.

13. If you wanted to calculate how many days it's been since someone purchased your product, which is the better option: have a cell that uses =TODAY() and then another cell that calculates days since purchase or just have a cell that calculates days since purchase and incorporates TODAY() into the formula? Why?
It's better to have the TODAY() function in its own cell so that all assumptions are visible. This way you can confirm that the worksheet updated when you opened it. Also, there will be times when someone isn't expecting the worksheet to have updated so having that visible makes it obvious what's happened.

TOP 10 FUNCTIONS – PART 3

1. What are the two base functions you could use if you want to write a formula that returns one result if X is true and another if it isn't?

IF or IFS

2. Write a formula that applies a 10% discount for any customer who buys at least $100 in merchandise assuming that the purchase amount is listed in Cell A1.

There are a number of ways to write this. Here are a few:

=IF(A1<100,A1,A1*0.9)
=IF(A1>=100,A1*0.9,A1)
=IFS(A1>=100,A1*0.9,TRUE,A1)

Note that here I turned the discount amount of 10% into 90%. Another way to write this would be with (1-CELL) where CELL was the cell that contained the discount amount. And since that would show assumptions, it's probably the better way to write that. Here an example putting the discount value in Cell B1 as a %.

=IFS(A1>=100,A1*(1-B1),TRUE,A1)

3. Explain what this formula is doing:
=IFS(B7>=B2,C2,B7>=B1,C1,TRUE,0)

It's saying that if the value in Cell B7 is greater than or equal to the value in Cell B2, return the value in Cell C2. If that's not the case then if the value in Cell B7 is greater than or equal to the value in Cell B1 return the value in Cell C1. If neither condition is true, return a value of 0.

4. What is one trick you can use when you get stuck building a complex formula that uses multiple if conditions?

Draw it out on a piece of paper. Show where you started and then draw the branches for the different outcomes and be sure to build each branch into your formula.

5. What does the AND function do?

Checks to see if all arguments are true or not. If so, it returns TRUE. If not, it returns FALSE.

6. What is =AND(A1>5,A2>4) asking?

It's asking if it's true that the value in Cell A1 is greater than five and also that the value in Cell A2 is greater than 4.

7. What is =AND(A1>B1,A2>B2) asking?

It's asking if the value in Cell A1 is greater than the value in Cell B1 and also if the value in Cell A2 is also greater than the value in Cell B2.

8. What is =IF(AND(A1="Jones",B1="Whatsit"), C1,D1) doing?

It's saying that if the value in Cell A1 is Jones and the value in Cell B1 is Whatsit then return the value in Cell C1, otherwise return the value in Cell D1.

9. What does VLOOKUP do?

Looks for a value in the leftmost column of a cell range and then returns a value in the same row of that cell range for the column you specify.

10. What must you do if you're using VLOOKUP on a table?

Sort your data using the values in the first column.

11. What's the best use for VLOOKUP?

Finding values in a reference table that's built to be used with the function.

12. Do the values in a reference table need to be an exact match for the value you're looking for when using VLOOKUP?

No.

13. With VLOOKUP can the column that has the values you're looking up be located anywhere in your data?

No. It must be the left-most column in the range you specify. It doesn't have to be the left-most column in your data but it must be the left-most column in the range and it must be to the left of the column with the values you want to return or be the same as that column.

14. How do you tell Excel whether to look for an exact match or an approximate match?

With the fourth element of your function. If you say TRUE or 1, it will look for an approximate match. If you say FALSE or 0, it will look for an exact match only.

15. What is the difference between an exact match and an approximate match?

An exact match will only return a result when what you're looking for is an exact match to an entry in the data table. An approximate match will return the result that's closest to the value you're looking for.

16. What is =VLOOKUP(25,A1:E10,3,FALSE) saying to do?

Lookup the value of 25 in Column A of a cell range that starts in Cell A1 and ends in Cell E10. If there is a value of 25 in Column A then return the value in the row that contains that value of 25 from Column C.

17. What is =VLOOKUP(25,A1:E10,2,TRUE) saying to do?

Lookup the value of 25 in Column A of a cell range that starts in Cell A1 and ends in Cell E10. Find the row in Column A of the table that is either equal to 25 or directly before the first row that has a value of more than 25 and return the value in Column B of that row.

18. What do you need to be careful of when using VLOOKUP with apparent numbers or dates?

If the numbers or dates are stored as text, they may produce unexpected results.

19. What should you always do when using any function in Excel?

Test to make sure that the result you get makes sense.

THE BASE FUNCTIONS

1. Write a formula that uses a function to calculate the average of the numeric values in Cells A1 through A5.

=AVERAGE(A1:A5)

Technically you could also use =SUM(A1:A5)/5 or =AVERAGEA(A1:A5) but they may give different results if the values in all of the cells are not numbers.

2. How would that calculation work if one of the cells in the range where you are trying to take an average is blank?

If you use the AVERAGE or AVERAGEA functions, Excel will ignore the blank cell. So it will sum the other four values and divide by four. It will not divide by five even though there were five cells in the specified range.

If you used SUM to calculate your average, it would still divide by 5.

3. What can you do to make sure that Excel includes all cells within the specified range when taking an average?

Put a zero in any blank cells so that they're included in the calculation.

Or use SUM and specify the number of cells to divide by yourself. (Although this won't scale well if the number of cells is variable.)

4. When using the AVERAGE function, what happens if one of the cells in your average range contains text?

Excel will ignore it. If you have a range of five cells and one has text in it, Excel will sum the values in the other four cells and divide by four.

5. What can you do to make sure that Excel includes cells with text in them when calculating an average over a range of cells?

Use the AVERAGEA function instead. It will treat text entries and FALSE values as having a value of 0 and TRUE values as having a value of 1.

Using the SUM function would work as well but you'd have to specify the number to divide by.

6. Can you take an average of the returns of a TRUE/FALSE series of responses to get the overall percent of responses that were true? How?

Yes. Using the AVERAGEA function.

7. If I have four cells with the values 2, 6, Other, and Now, what result will I get using AVERAGE? What result will I get using AVERAGEA?

AVERAGE will return a result of 4 which is 2+6 divided by 2. AVERAGEA will return a result of 2 which is 2+6 divided by 4.

8. What does the COUNT function allow you to do?
It allows you to count how many cells within the specified range have a number or date in them.

9. Does COUNT include cells with text in them?
No.

10. Does COUNT include cells with formulas in them that create a number or date?
Yes.

11. Does COUNT include cells with formulas in them that create a text entry?
No.

12. If a cell contains "1 unit" as its value, will COUNT count it?
No.

13. Write a formula using COUNT on a range of cells from B2 through D8.
=COUNT(B2:D8)

14. What function can you use if you also want to count cells that contain text in them?
COUNTA

15. What does this function allow you to do?
Count all cells in the range that are not empty.

16. What happens when you have a function in a cell, say =CONCATENATE(A1,B1,C1) but that cell is currently not displaying a value and you use each of the count functions?

COUNT will not count the cell. COUNTA will.

17. What should you always do when using any function?

Test to make sure that it's doing what you think it should be, including testing the COUNT functions to make sure that the cells you want counted are being counted.

18. What does COUNTBLANK do?

It counts the number of cells in the range that are empty but this can include cells that have a formula in it that is currently not returning a value.

19. If you have an issue with which cells are being counted by a specific count function, what should you do?

Look to the nature of the cells in question. Perhaps they look blank but have a space in them or they look blank but contain a function.

20. If you want the minimum value within a range, what function can you use to get it?

MIN or MINA

21. If you want the maximum value within a range, what function can you use to get it?

MAX or MAXA

22. How would you write the formula to calculate the minimum value in Column D?

=MIN(D:D) or =MINA(D:D)

23. How would you write the formula to calculate the maximum value in Row 3?

=MAX(3:3) or =MAXA(3:3)

24. What value will Excel return if you ask for the minimum or maximum of a range of values that have no numbers in them?

0

25. What will happen if you try to take the minimum or maximum of a range of values that has an error value in it such as #DIV/0!?

It will return the error value.

26. If you have a range of values that you want to take a minimum of but that range includes TRUE and FALSE entries that you want included in the calculation, what function should you use?

MINA

27. How do MINA and MAXA treat TRUE or FALSE values?

TRUE values are treated as a 1. FALSE values are treated as a 0.

28. How do MINA and MAXA treat text?

A text entry is treated as a zero.

29. What result will you get from =MINA(A1:A3) where A1 is the word Other, A2 is 2, and A3 is 3? What about =MIN(A1:A3)?

MINA will return a value of 0 but MIN will return a value of 2.

30. What result will you get from =MINA(A1:A3) where A1 is -2, A2 is 2, and A3 is 3? What about =MIN(A1:A3)?

Both will return a value of -2.

31. What result will you get from =MAXA(A1:A3) where A1 is -2, A2 is 2, and A3 is 3? What about =MAX(A1:A3)?

Both will return a value of 3.

32. What result will you get from =MAXA(A1:A3) where A1 is -2, A2 is 2, and A3 is Title? What about =MAX(A1:A3)?

Both will return a value of 2.

THE LOGICAL* FUNCTIONS

1. What does the OR function do?

Checks to see if any of the arguments listed are true. If so, it returns TRUE. If not, it returns FALSE.

2. What is =OR(A1>5,A2>4) asking?

If either the value in Cell A1 is greater than five or the value in Cell A2 is greater than 4.

3. What is =IF(OR(A1="Canton",B1="Toledo"), G1,G1*2) doing?

It's saying that if the value in Cell A1 is either Canton or Toledo then return the value in Cell G1. If it isn't, then return a value equal to the value in Cell G1 times two.

4. What do the TRUE and FALSE functions do?

They return a value of TRUE or FALSE.

5. When might you use them?

When you're using functions that return different

results for a TRUE or FALSE result. Sometimes simply typing TRUE or FALSE doesn't create the same result as using the TRUE() and FALSE() functions. For example, say you wanted to use AVERAGEA on the results of an IF function. You could have the IF function return a result of TRUE or FALSE and then apply AVERAGEA to those results to see how many times on average the conditions were met.

6. What does the NA function do?
Returns the error value #N/A.

7. When might you use the NA function?
To mark empty cells when using a formula. If you return an empty space instead of an N/A result some functions won't work properly. This can be especially useful when having to graph results since Excel will not graph N/A values whereas it will graph empty results.

8. What do you need to remember when using the TRUE, FALSE, or NA functions?
That you always need to include the parens after the function name. So write TRUE() not TRUE.

9. What functions is the NOT function related to?
The AND and OR functions.

10. Why do I encourage you to find a way to use a function other than the NOT function to build a formula?
Because using a negative to build a formula is counter to how most people think.

11. What result will you get if you use =NOT(FALSE)?

    TRUE

THE IF FUNCTIONS

1. What do you need to be aware of when using the various IF functions if someone with an older version of Excel might use your worksheet?

Older versions of Excel did not include all of the IF Functions that Excel 2019 includes. For example, MINIFS, MAXIFS, and IFS were all new in Excel 2019. Also, some even older versions of Excel don't include SUMIFS, AVERAGEIFS, or COUNTIFS they only include SUMIF, AVERAGEIF, and COUNTIF.

2. What function would you use if you had a table of sales data and wanted to know the average transaction amount for customers in Montana who bought Whatsits?

AVERAGEIFS

(You could probably also use a combination of AVERAGE with the IF or IFS function using an AND function.)

3. Write a formula that takes the average of the values in Column C when the values in Column A are "MT" and the values in Column B are "Whatsits" and the data to be used is in Rows 1 through 6.

=AVERAGEIFS(C1:C6,A1:A6,"MT",B1:B6,"Whatsits")

(You could also do this by having a calculation for each row using =IF(AND(A1="MT",B1="Whatsits"),C1,"") and then taking the average of the values returned in the calculation column but AVERAGEIFS is much simpler to use.

4. What function would you use if you had a table of sales data and wanted to know the number of transaction where customers in Montana bought Whatsits?

COUNTIFS

5. Write a formula that counts the number of results where the value in Column A is "MT" and the value in Column B is "Whatsits" and the data to be used is in Rows 1 through 6.

=COUNTIFS(A1:A6,"MT",B1:B6,"Whatsits")

6. What function would you use if you had a table of sales data and wanted to sum the amount that customers in Montana who bought Whatsits have spent?

SUMIFS

7. Write a formula that sums the amount that customers spent where amount spent is listed in Column C and the values in Column A are "MT" and the values in Column

B are "Whatsits" and the data to be used is in Rows 1 through 6.

=SUMIFS(C1:C6,A1:A6,"MT",B1:B6,"Whatsits")

8. What function would you use if you had a table of sales data and wanted to know the minimum amount any customer from Montana who bought Whatsits spent? What function would you use if you wanted to know the maximum amount spent.

MINIFS

MAXIFS

9. Write a formula that finds the minimum amount spent when transaction amount is in Column C for cases where the value in Column A was "MT" and the value in Column B was "Whatsits" and the data to be used is in Rows 1 through 6.

=MINIFS(C1:C6,A1:A6,"MT",B1:B6,"Whatsits")

10. What is one way to troubleshoot a complex IF or IFS function that involves multiple conditions?

Break the formula down into one condition at a time by replacing the rest of the function with filler text. So instead of a lengthy IF function with multiple conditions, have =IF(A1>10,"THEN",0) where "THEN" has been used to replace the rest of the function so that you can see if the initial condition and the final outcome are written as they should be.

Once that portion of the function has been confirmed to work, drop it away and move to the next condition.

11. With an IF function that has multiple conditions, what should you always check for?

That there are as many closing parens as opening parens and that they are in the right location.

12. Use IF to write a formula that looks at the value in Cell A1 and if it is greater than 10 returns a result of A, if it is greater than 5 and up to a value of 10 returns a result of B, and if it is 5 or less returns a value of C. Write the same formula using IFS.
    =IF(A1>10,"A",IF(A1>5,"B","C"))
    =IFS(A1>10,"A",A1>5,"B",TRUE,"C")

13. If you want to count how many times the values in Cells C10 through C25 are greater than the value in Cell A1, how would you write that?
    =COUNTIFS(C10:C25,">"&A1)

14. What do you need to watch out for when using COUNTIFS, SUMIFS, AVERAGEIFS, MINIFS, and MAXIFS?
    That your cell ranges for each of your criteria are properly lined up. If your data is stored across columns then you want to make sure your data starts with the same row number for all criteria, for example, so that Excel is looking at the values for the criteria in those columns across the same row. (Assuming that's how your data is set up. As long as the cell ranges are the same size, Excel can work with it, but remember, garbage in, garbage out.)

15. What do the asterisk (*), the question mark (?), and the tilde (~) represent when you're writing a count, sum, average, min, or max criteria?
    The asterisk is a wildcard that represents any number of characters. The question mark is a wildcard that represents

one single character. The tilde is a symbol you can use before an asterisk or question mark to indicate that that's actually what you wanted to search for rather than it being a wild card.

16. With COUNTIFS, SUMIFS, AVERAGEIFS, MINIFS, and MAXIFS if you have three criteria you specify and two of the three are met, what will happen with that entry?

It will not be included in the calculation. All of the criteria you specify must be met for Excel to count the entry or include its value in the calculation.

17. Why is this important?

Because if you write one of your criteria wrong, your function is not going to work properly. Remember to test, test, test your function, especially along the borders. So if your criteria is all entries over 100, test 101 and 100 to see what result you get.

18. What function can you use to suppress an #N/A! result in a formula?

The IFNA function.

19. Apply that function to the following formula: =VLOOKUP(D:D,'Advertising Spend By Series'!E:F,2,FALSE) so that a value of 0 is returned instead of the #N/A! error message.

=IFNA(VLOOKUP(D:D,'Advertising Spend By Series'!E:F,2,FALSE),0)

20. Now apply the function to the following formula: =VLOOKUP(D:D,'Advertising Spend By Series'!E:F,

2,FALSE)so that a value of **"No Match"** is returned
instead of the #N/A! error message.

=IFNA(VLOOKUP(D:D,'Advertising Spend By
Series'!E:F,2,FALSE),"No Match")

**21. And also apply the function to the following
formula: =VLOOKUP(D:D,'Advertising Spend By
Series'!E:F,2,FALSE) so that a blank value is
returned instead of the #N/A! error message.**

=IFNA(VLOOKUP(D:D,'Advertising Spend By
Series'!E:F,2,FALSE),"")

**22. What function can you use to suppress all error
messages instead of just #N/A!?**

The IFERROR function.

**23. Apply that function to a situation where you are
dividing the value in Cell A1 by the value in Cell B1
and you want to return a blank result instead of an
error message.**

=IFERROR(A1/B1,"")

**24. Now apply that function to a situation where you
are dividing the value in Cell A1 by the value in Cell
B1 and you want to return a value of "Error" instead
of a specific error message.**

=IFERROR(A1/B1,"Error")

25. What is the danger in using IFNA or IFERROR?

They may suppress a legitimate error message that you
need to see. A #N/A! error can indicate that you have, for
example, a formatting or spelling error in a list of values.
And a #DIV/0! error can indicate you're missing a value

you thought you had or that you're using the wrong cell in your equation.

26. What is one way of addressing this issue?

Have the formula return a text value instead of a value of zero or a blank value. This will indicate that an error message was generated by the calculation so that you can properly review it without interfering with any calculations on those cells.

THE LOOKUP FUNCTIONS – PART 1

1. What does the HLOOKUP function do?

It scans across a row of data to match a value you specify and then pulls a result from another row in the same column where that match was made.

For example, you could scan for a month in a table with month values across the top and then pull the specific result for a vendor if vendor results were listed in rows below each month.

2. What will this formula do:
=HLOOKUP("April",B1:M12,4,FALSE)

It will look for a cell with the value "April" in row one of the data set contained in Cells B1 through M12 and then will go to the fourth row of that column and pull the value in the corresponding cell. In this case, a value will only be returned if there is an exact match to "April".

3. What can you look up using HLOOKUP?

A numeric value, a text string, or a cell reference.

4. If you look up a text string, what do you need to be sure to do?

Put quotation marks around the text string you want to look up.

5. What are wildcards and how can you use them when looking up text?

A wildcard, like * or ?, allows you to look up text without being exact about what text you're looking up. For example, "*April" would look up any text string that has April at the very end no matter how long the text string. So it would include "I like the month of April" as a valid match. On the other hand, "?April" will look for any text string that has one character before April. So "1April" would be a valid match but "20th April" would not.

6. In the table you're going to search using HLOOKUP, where do the values you're searching for need to be?

The first row of the range specified in the function.

7. In the table you're going to search using HLOOKUP, where do the values you want to return need to be?

In the lookup row or in the rows below the lookup row.

8. What is the difference between using FALSE and TRUE as the final criteria for the HLOOKUP function?

Using FALSE means that only an exact match will return a value. Using TRUE will return an approximate value.

9. What is the risk to using TRUE as the third input to the HLOOKUP function?

If your data isn't sorted in ascending order before you use the function, the value returned may not be the closest value.

10. Can you sort the values in a row in ascending order?

Yes. It's an option under the Sort function in Excel. Choose the Sort Left to Right option.

11. When you tell Excel which row to pull your result from using HLOOKUP, what number do you need to provide? Is it the Row number in the worksheet or something else?

No, it is not the row number in the worksheet. It's the row within the cell range specified in the HLOOKUP function.

12. If you provide a row value of 1 in the HLOOKUP function what will that return assuming there is a result to return?

Either the value you were looking for if you were looking for an exact match (FALSE) or the closest value if you were looking for an approximate value (TRUE).

13. If you ask HLOOKUP to find an exact match and there isn't one, what value will Excel return?

#N/A!

14. What could potentially result in an incorrect error message when using HLOOKUP?

A spelling error in the formula, extra spaces in the entries that are being looked at, an incorrect table range, incorrect row references, or a lookup value outside the range in the table.

15. What does the SWITCH function do?

It allows you to provide up to 126 different responses based upon the result of a calculation.

16. Write a formula using the SWITCH function that tells someone they are correct if the value in Cell A1 is 50 and incorrect if it's any other value.

=SWITCH(A1,50,"Correct","Incorrect")

17. Write a formula using the SWITCH function that assigns all Grade 9 students to A Rotation, all Grade 10 students to B Rotation, all Grade 11 students to C Rotation, and all Grade 12 students to D Rotation, assuming that Cell A1 contains the grade number. Include a condition for when a student is not listed with a grade or listed with a grade other than 9, 10, 11, or 12.

=SWITCH(A1,9,"A Rotation",10,"B Rotation",11,"C Rotation",12,"D Rotation","No Grade Specified or Incorrect Grade")

18. If you were using the SWITCH function and anticipated that your assignments (such as A Rotation, etc.) were going to change over time, what is one way to build the formula so that it is easier to modify it later?

Use cell references in the formula itself and keep the data that might change in a separate table. So in the example above you'd have one column of the table with Grade and one with Rotation and any change made to the values in that table would also update the results of the SWITCH formula for all rows.

19. What does the CHOOSE function do?

It lets you pick a result from a list of values based upon the index number.

20. When is CHOOSE most powerful?

When combined with another function or calculation that provides the index number.

21. What will the result be of =CHOOSE(3,1,2,3) be? Why?

3. Because that's saying to choose the third value in the list which is also 3.

THE LOOKUP FUNCTIONS – PART 2

1. What does the TRANSPOSE function do?

It converts a vertical range of cells to a horizontal range or vice versa. In other words, it take a range of values in a row and puts them in a column or takes a range of values in a column and puts them in a row instead.

2. Does TRANSPOSE work on a table of values that covers multiple rows and/or columns?

Yes.

3. What do you have to do special because TRANSPOSE is an array formula?

Two things. You must first select the range of cells where you want your result to go before you start typing your formula in the first cell of the range. And you must also use Ctrl+Shift+Enter when you finish entering the formula (rather than just Enter) for it to work.

4. If you want to take the values in Cells C1 through C5 and place them in Cells E8 through I8, how would you do that?

Highlight Cells E8 through I8. Type in the formula =TRANSPOSE(C1:C5) in Cell E8 (while keeping the other cells highlighted). Finish with Ctrl+Shift+Enter.

5. If all you want to do is change the orientation of your data but not keep a reference to the original cells, what is a better option?

Use Copy and Paste-Transpose instead.

6. What is the difference between using the TRANSPOSE function and using Paste-Transpose?

When you use the TRANSPOSE function the values in your cells are still linked to their original source, so a change in the value in the original location will change the transposed value as well. When you use Copy and Paste-Transpose those pasted values are now separate from the original source values.

7. What are the two tasks that the INDEX function can perform?

It can either return a single value from a specified position in a table or it can return a range of values from a specified position in a table.

8. What is the following formula supposed to do: =INDEX(A2:E7,3,4)

Return the value in the third row of the fourth column of the data composed of Cells A2 through E7 which is the value in Cell D4.

9. Does the INDEX function require you to include a header row or row labels in the specified cell range?

No, but when specifying the row and column number for the value you want you should take into account whether the header row or row labels are part of the cell range.

10. How do you determine the row number value to use in the INDEX function?

It should be the number that corresponds to the order of the row within the defined range. It is not the actual row number in the Excel worksheet.

11. How do you determine the column number value to use in the INDEX function?

It should be the number that corresponds to the order of the column within the defined range. It is not the actual column number in the Excel worksheet.

12. Can you use the INDEX function with more than one table of data? How?

Yes. There is an optional fourth variable that can be included in the INDEX function that specifies which data table to pull the value from. In order to use it you have to provide multiple table ranges in the first input.

13. What happens if you use the fourth variable in the INDEX function without providing multiple table range values in the first variable?

You will get a #REF! error message.

14. If you want to use the INDEX function to pull an entire column or row of data, what do you need to do?

Use the function as an array formula. This means you highlight the cells where you want that data to go first, enter the formula in the first cell of that highlighted range, and then use Ctrl+Shift+Enter instead of Enter when you're done.

To pull an entire column leave the row variable blank or set it to zero. To pull an entire row leave the column variable blank or set it to zero.

For example,

=INDEX(A2:E7,2,)

and

=INDEX(A2:E7,,3)

will pull the entire second row and entire third column, respectively.

15. Can you easily copy and paste an array formula?

No.

16. Once you've extracted values from a table using the INDEX function are the results fixed values?

No. This is still a formula, so it's still pulling those values from the source table and any changes to the source table will change the values you pulled. The only way to fix the values is to then take the results and Copy and Paste Special-Values to remove the formula but keep the values.

17. What does the MATCH function do?

It returns the relative position of an item in a specified range of cells. It can also return the relative position of the closest value if there is no exact match in the range of cells as long as the values in the cells are properly sorted.

18. If the MATCH function returns a value of 2 for the following formula, what does that mean: =MATCH($A12,$A$2:$A$7,0)

That an exact match to the value in Cell A12 is in the second row of the data in the range from Cell A2 through Cell A7. The first value is the value you're looking for, the second is the range of cells where that value may be, and the third value says that it should be an exact match.

19. What is the value in using the MATCH function?

It can be combined with other functions, like the INDEX function to facilitate looking up values in data tables.

20. What kinds of values can MATCH look for?

Numeric, text values, or logical values.

21. What are the three match types that you can use with MATCH?

You can look for an exact match, the smallest value that is greater than or equal to the specified value, or the largest value that is less than or equal to the specified value.

22. If you're not looking for an exact match what do you need to do first? And how will your choice of match type impact this?

You need to sort your data. If you're looking for the smallest value that is greater than the specified value sort in descending order. If you're looking for the largest value that is less than the specified value sort in ascending order.

23. What is the default match type used by MATCH? Why is this a problem?

If you don't specify a match type (-1,0,1) then Excel will assume you wanted to use the 1 match type and will look for the largest value that is less than or equal to the specified value. This is a problem if you haven't sorted your data to accommodate that type of match.

24. Is the value returned by MATCH the row number or the column number in the worksheet or something else?

It is not the row or column number in the worksheet. It is the relative row number or relative column number within the specified cell range.

THE STATISTICAL FUNCTIONS

1. What is the difference between an average, a mean, and a mode?

An average is an arithmetic mean of a series of numbers. It's calculated by adding those numbers together and then dividing by the count of the numbers you just added. So if I average 3, 4, and 5, the result is 4 because I add 3, 4, and 5 to get 12 and then divide by 3 to get 4.

The median value is the number in the middle of a range of values. Looking at the example above with 3, 4, and 5 the median value is also 4 because it's the middle value.

The mode returns the most frequently occurring or repetitive value in a range. It's basically telling you where there's a bump in your data. It's especially useful in situations where there is a heavy concentration of values and that concentration of values is not in the center of the range.

2. What's a good idea when dealing with a large range of data points that will help you figure out whether average, mean, or mode works best for your data?

Plot it. If you put your data points onto a scatter plot you will be able to see if there are any unusual concentrations in the data points or any sort of skew to your data that could impact the result of using average, mean, or mode.

3. How would you write the function to calculate the median of a range of values from Cells C1 through C9?
=MEDIAN(C1:C9)

4. How does Excel calculate the median when there is an even number of values in the range?
It averages the middle two values.

5. Why can this be dangerous?
Because if you have data that's something like 1, 1, 100, 100, Excel will return a value of 50.5 even though that value is nowhere close to an actual value in the data.

6. What function should you use to find the most common result when your data has a large bump or bumps that aren't near the midline?
MODE.SNGL or MODE.MULT.

7. How would you write this function for a range of values in Cells B2 through B10 where you just have one bump in the data?
=MODE.SNGL(B2:B10)

8. What is special about the MODE.MULT function?
It's an array formula which means it returns results in more than one cell.

9. How do you use MODE.MULT?

Highlight the range of cells where you want Excel to return your results. If there are two bumps in the data, highlight two cells. If there are three, highlight three cells, etc. Only once you've done this should you type in your MODE.MULT function with the cell range you want to evaluate. And then, instead of hitting Enter, use Ctrl + Shift + Enter.

10. If you've properly used MODE.MULT, what will it look like in the formula bar when you click back into the cell for the function?

It will have curvy brackets at each end like this: {=MODE.MULT(A1:A10)}

11. If you have multi-modal data where two values occur with the same high frequency but you use the MODE.SNGL or MODE function instead of the MODE.MULT function, what will happen?

Excel will return the first value that occurs at that frequency. So if 5 and 25 both occur at an equally frequent high amount in the data, Excel will only return the 5 value.

12. What can you do if you want your MODE.MULT results to display in a row instead of in a column?

Combine it with the TRANSPOSE function. For example, =TRANSPOSE(MODE.MULT(A1:A10))

13. What is one issue with MODE.MULT that you're still going to run into?

It's only going to return the most frequently occurring results. So if you have one value that occurs 10 times, another that occurs 10 times, and a third that occurs 9 times it will only return those first two values even though that third one may also be of interest to you.

14. How could you work around this issue?
Build a count table of your values that counts each value and its number of occurrences and then sort by count to see your top values that way.

15. What function or functions can you use if you want to know the rank of a specific value within a range of possible values? In other words, is this the 5th largest number, the 10th, the 20th, etc. compared to other numbers in the range?
RANK, RANK.EQ, or RANK.AVG

16. If you want to know the rank of a value in Cell A1 from within the range of Cells A1 through A15, how can you write that function using ascending values? What about descending values?
Ascending:
=RANK.EQ(A1,A1:A15,1)
or =RANK.AVG(A1,A1:A15,1)
or =RANK(A1,A1:A15,1)
Descending:
=RANK.EQ(A1,A1:A15)
or =RANK.AVG(A1,A1:A15)
or =RANK(A1,A1:A15,0)
or =RANK(A1,A1:A15)

17. To use one of the ranking functions does your data have to be sorted?
No.

18. How do RANK.EQ and RANK.AVG differ?

In how they treat instances where there is more than one of a result. For RANK.EQ all ties are assigned the highest possible rank for that value and then Excel skips however many ranks it needs to. For RANK.AVG Excel takes the possible ranks for those tied values and returns an average for the ranks.

19. What does the SMALL function do?

Returns the k-th smallest value in a data set where you specify the value of k.

20. What does the LARGE function do?

Returns the k-th largest value in a data set where you specify the value of k.

21. Can you technically use SMALL to return the largest value in a range and LARGE to return the smallest value in a range?

Yes. As long as you know the size of your range and use a k that's equal to that number.

22. What does the FORECAST.LINEAR function do?

It calculates a value for y given a specified value for x and existing known values for x and y. Predictions are made assuming a linear trend.

23. Why is it important to remember that it only works with a linear trend?

Because many relationships that occur in life are not in fact linear and so the forecasted value will not necessarily be accurate.

24. Because of this, what should you do before using the FORECAST function?

Plot your data to see if it's following a linear or near linear trend. If it isn't, don't use FORECAST.LINEAR.

25. What are the order of the inputs to the FORECAST.LINEAR function?

You list the x you want Excel to use in its prediction, then a range for all of the known y values, and then a corresponding range for all of the known x values.

26. Does your data need to be sorted to use FORECAST.LINEAR?

No.

27. What does the FREQUENCY function do?

It takes a list of values and calculates how many occurrences of those values fall within ranges specified by the user.

28. What must you have in order to use the FREQUENCY function?

A series of "bin" values for the function to use so that it knows how to define each range.

29. What does it mean that FREQUENCY is an array function?

That it will return more than one value. This means that you have to highlight the cells where you want your answers returned first, then you type the formula in the first cell of the range, and then you use Ctrl+Shift+Enter to finish the calculation.

30. What are the inputs to the FREQUENCY function?

Data Array: This is the range of cells that include the data whose frequency you want to calculate.

Bins Array: This is the range of cells that define the bins you want to use for the calculation.

31. How is a bins array entry structured? And how is it used by Excel?

Each bin in the array is a single numeric value entered in a cell. For the first cell in a bins array, Excel will calculate the number of cells in the data array that have a value less than or equal to that value. For the next cell it will calculate the number of cells that have a value greater than the last one but less than or equal to the current cell. And so on. The final bins array, if it's blank will be used to calculate any entries greater than the last specified value.

32. What is an easy way to get a list of bin array values that correspond to all potential values in your data set?

Copy and paste those values into a new range and then use the Remove Duplicates option under Data Tools in the Data tab to get a list of unique values from the original range.

33. If the range of values you want to evaluate are in Column C and your bins values are in Cells D2 through D6, how would you write the formula to calculate your frequencies for each of those bin values?

=FREQUENCY(C:C,D2:D6)

MORE MATH FUNCTIONS

1. If you had a table of data that contained customer in Column A, units bought by that customer in Column B, and price per unit in Column C and wanted to get a total spent for all customers using one function, what function could you use? How would you write it.

SUMPRODUCT

=SUMPRODUCT(B:B,C:C)

2. When using this function, what does the #VALUE! error message likely indicate?

That the arrays (or cell ranges) that you provided for the function are not the same size.

3. What does Excel do with text entries included in the cell range for that function?

Treats the text as a zero which means it will return a zero result for any line where one of the entries is text.

4. What function would you use to take the absolute value of a number?

ABS

5. Write a formula to take the absolute value of -3:

=ABS(-3)

6. What function can be used to raise a number to a power? For example, to take the number 3 to the 2nd power. Write that formula.

POWER

=POWER(3,2)

7. Is there a way to do this without a function? How?

Yes. The carat ^ will do the same thing. So =3^2 will return the same result.

8. Can you use both of these methods to take a root power, such as the square root of a number? If so, write how to take the square root of 9.

Yes. =POWER(9,.5) or =9^.5

You could also use (1/2) instead of .5 in either of the above formulas.

9. Is there a function that will specifically let you take the square root of a number? What is it? Apply it to 9.

Yes. SQRT.

=SQRT(9)

10. How can you derive the value of e using a function?

=EXP(1)

11. What is the function that will let you return the value of Pi to fifteen digits? How would you write it?

PI

=PI()

12. What is =LOG(100) asking?

It's asking what power you'd have to take the number 10 to in order to get a value of 100. In this case, the answer is 2.

13. Write a formula that uses the LOG function to determine what power you'd have to take the number 2 to in order to get a result of 24:

=LOG(24,2)

14. Write a formula that uses the LOG function to determine what power you'd have to take e to in order to get a result of 24:

=LOG(24,EXP(1))

15. Write a formula that uses the LN function to make the same determination:

=LN(24)

16. What formula would you write to determine the number of possible permutations for a group of ten people?

=FACT(10)

17. What happens with the FACT function if you input a decimal value, for example =FACT(3.95)?

It will truncate the number provided and then do the factorial calculation. So in this case it would return the equivalent of =FACT(3).

18. What happens if you ask for the factorial of a negative number?

You'll get a #NUM! error message.

19. What function would you use if you wanted to calculate the number of three-person teams that could be built out of a population of nine people. How would you write that?

COMBIN
=COMBIN(9,3)

20. What function would you use to determine the total number of possible outcomes for a group of nine people where you were assigning three prizes and each person in the group was allowed to win each prize even if they'd already won? How would you write that?

COMBINA
=COMBINA(9,3)

THE TEXT FUNCTIONS

1. If you want to convert a text string into uppercase letters, which function should you use?
UPPER

2. What if you want to convert a text string into lowercase letters?
LOWER

3. What if you want the initial letter of each word to be capitalized, but the rest to be in lowercase?
PROPER

4. Let's say that you have a text string in Cell C10 and another in Cell C11 and that you want to combine those entries with a space between them and convert them into uppercase letters. How could you do that?
One solution would be:
=UPPER(TEXTJOIN(" ",1,C10,C11))

5. What does the LEFT function do? What does the RIGHT function do?

LEFT returns the first x number of characters from the left-hand side of a text string. RIGHT returns the first x characters from the right-hand side of a text string.

6. If you want to return the first five characters of the text in Cell A1, how would you do that?

=LEFT(A1,5)

7. Do these functions work with numbers as well?

Yes.

8. What happens if the number of characters you specify is greater than the number of characters in the string you reference?

Excel returns the entire result.

9. What happens if you don't specify a number of characters to return?

Excel will default to a value of 1 and just return the first character.

10. What does the MID function do?

It returns the specified number of characters from a text string given a starting position within that text string.

11. What happens if the start point you provide for the MID function is greater than the number of characters in the string?

Excel returns an empty result.

12. What happens if you use MID and ask Excel to return more characters than there are in the text string?

It will return what there is.

13. What other function could you use to get the same result as =MID(A1,1,2)?

=LEFT(A1,2)

14. What does Excel say that the TEXT function can do?

Convert a value to text in a specific number format.

15. What else can the TEXT function actually do?

Extract information from a date. You can use TEXT to return the day of the week, month of the year, or a time component from a date. And with day of the week or month of the year that will be the written form of the date, so December or Dec, for example.

16. If you have a date in Cell A1 and want to pull the full name of the day of the week, how would you do that using the TEXT function?

=TEXT(A1,"dddd")

17. What about the month of the year?

=TEXT(A1,"mmmm")

18. What does the LEN function do?

It returns the number of characters in a text string.

19. What result would LEN return for =LEN("This one")? Why?

8. Because it includes the space between "this" and "one" in the count of length.

20. How does LEN handle a formula in a cell?

It returns a count of the length of the result of the formula. So if the formula returned a value of 8, then LEN would return a value of 1 in reference to that cell.

21. What is the following formula doing: =LEFT(A1,LEN(A1)-LEN(" units"))?

It's taking the left n-most characters from Cell A1 where n is equal to the total number of characters in Cell A1 minus the number of characters in " units". This is a way to extract the numeric value from an entry such as 12,000 units or 500 units where the number of characters in the numeric portion of the value is an unknown.

22. What does the EXACT function do?

It returns a value of TRUE or FALSE based upon whether two text strings are exactly the same or not.

23. Is EXACT case-sensitive?

Yes. It will return a value of FALSE if used on "This" and "this", for example.

THE DATE & TIME FUNCTIONS

1. When converted to a date what does the number 1 represent in Excel?

The date January 1, 1900.

2. Can Excel handle dates prior to that date?

No.

3. Can you use addition and subtraction with dates in Excel? Why or why not?

Yes. Because each date in Excel is stored as a number, you can use addition and subtraction with dates in Excel.

4. If you enter a two-digit year, for example '29, how will Excel treat that in terms of the century it applies?

For two-digit years between 00 and 29 it will interpret that as a date set in the 2000s, so 2000 to 2029. For two-digit years between 30 and 99 it will treat that as a date set in the 1900s, so 1930 to 1999.

5. What does the DATE function do?

Creates a date using the year, month, and day inputs provided.

6. What happens if you use the DATE function with a date prior to January 1, 1900, so for example if you use =DATE(1880,1,1)?

Excel will add the year value you provided to 1900 to provide the date. So =DATE(1880,1,1) becomes 1/1/3780.

7. Can you use a value for the month portion of the DATE function that is greater than 12? What about less than 1?

Yes. If you do so, Excel will take the year and day of the month provided and add that many months. If the number for months provided is negative it will subtract that many months, but it includes a value of zero as a legitimate month count. So =DATE(1905,-2,1) will go back to October 1, 1904 which is January minus three months.

8. What about days of the month? Can you have a number greater than 31 or a negative number?

Yes. It works the same way as the months do. It will carry forward that many days or if it goes backward it will go back that many days plus one additional day.

9. Write a formula that takes a date stored in Cell B2 and adds four months to it.

=DATE(YEAR(B2),MONTH(B2)+4,DAY(B2))

10. What does the YEAR function do?

It returns the year portion of a date in the integer range of 1900 through 9999.

11. How would you use YEAR to extract the year portion of the date March 1, 2010?

Possible examples:
=YEAR("March, 1, 2010")
=YEAR("3/1/2010")
=YEAR("3-1-2010")
=YEAR(A1) where A1 contains the date

12. What happens if you fail to use quotation marks around a date used in a YEAR function?

You will get a #NUM! error message.

13. What are the equivalent functions to year for month, day of the month, hour, minute of the day, and seconds? What kind of value will be returned for the hour?

MONTH, DAY, HOUR, MINUTE, SECOND

HOUR returns a value between 0 and 23 because it uses military time.

14. What does the WEEKDAY function do?

It returns the day of the week for a specified date using a value of 1 through 7 where the day of the week represented by each number is dependent upon the setting specified by the user.

15. What is the default setting for the WEEKDAY function in terms of numbering the days of the week?

By default, 1 will equal Sunday and so on until 7 equals Saturday.

16. If August 13, 2019 is a Tuesday and I use =WEEKDAY("August 13, 2019") what value will I get back?

   3

17. What portion of the WEEKDAY function should you change if you want the numbers returned to map to different days of the week? How would you change the above formula so that Monday is treated as a 1 and Tuesday returns a value of 2 instead?

The optional return_type variable lets you specify which day of the week is considered the first day of the week. To change =WEEKDAY("August 13, 2019") so that Monday is the first day of the week and any Tuesday is a value of 2 you would write =WEEKDAY("August 13, 2019",2) or =WEEKDAY("August 13, 2019",11)

18. What does the WEEKNUM function do? What is the highest value it will return?

It returns a number for which week in the year a date is part of. It returns values as high as 53.

19. How does Excel define a week for purposes of the WEEKNUM function?

That depends on the return_type you choose. The default is for Excel to define a week as starting on a Sunday but also to only include dates for that given year. So, for example, for 2019 week 1 started with January 1st, a Tuesday, through January 5th, a Saturday.

20. How do you get Excel to define a week in accordance with ISO standards when using the WEEKNUM function? And how does it work?

By setting the return_type value to 21. Excel takes the first week of the year that has a Thursday in it and starts the week on the Monday of that week even if the Monday of that week falls in the prior year.

21. What is another function you can use to get Excel to apply the ISO standard when determining the week number?
ISOWEEKNUM

22. What does the EDATE function do?
The EDATE function takes a date and gives the same date x number of months from that date. If the cell is not formatted as a date, it will return the value as a number.

23. What is another way to get this same result?
Use the DATE function to extract YEAR, MONTH, and DAY from a date and then add the desired number of months to the MONTH value.

24. If I use =EDATE("March 1, 2019",4) what result will that give me?
43647 which is equivalent to July 1, 2019 because it takes that date and moves only the month portion forward the specified number of months.

25. How does EDATE handle partial month values, such as =EDATE("March 1, 2019",4.9)?
It truncates the provided value, so this would be the equivalent of =EDATE("March 1, 2019",4)

26. What does the EOMONTH function do?
The EOMONTH function takes a date and gives the

date as of the end of a month x number of months from that date. If the cell is not formatted as a date, it will return the value as a number.

27. What does the NETWORKDAYS.INTL function do?

It allows you to calculate the number of whole workdays between two dates and lets you specify which days in a week should be considered workdays and which are not.

28. Explain what the weekend input to the NETWORKDAYS.INTL function does.

It allows you to specify a custom weekend parameter. You can have a "weekend" that is only one day of the week or a weekend that consists of any two continuous days within the week by using this input. The values are listed in a dropdown menu.

29. What does the WORKDAY.INTL function do? Is it directly interchangeable with NETWORKDAYS.INTL?

It returns the value for the date that is before or after a specified number of workdays but also allows for custom weekend parameters. It is not directly interchangeable with NETWORKDAYS.INTL because it does not include the current or final day in its calculations.

WHEN THINGS GO WRONG

1. Name five different error messages you might see.
#REF!, #VALUE!, #DIV/0!, #N/A, #NUM!

You also might see a comment that you've created a circular reference or have too few arguments or that the formula you've written doesn't work and Excel wants to fix it for you.

2. What does #REF! generally indicate?
That you've deleted a value that was being referenced in that cell. For example, =A1+B1 will generate that message if you delete Column A or Column B.

3. How can you see where the cell that was deleted was located in your formula?
Click on the cell and look in the formula bar or double-click on the cell. The cell reference that's missing will have been replaced with #REF!.

4. What does a #VALUE! message indicate?

That the cell you're referencing is the wrong type of cell for that function. So maybe you have a date or number formatted as plain text, for example. In rare cases it could also mean that you have regional settings that impact how you're supposed to write your functions. It can also mean that you're referencing a now unavailable outside data source.

5. What does a #DIV/0! message indicate?

That you're dividing by zero or a blank cell.

6. What does a #N/A error message generally mean?

That Excel isn't finding what it was asked to look for.

7. What can you check for if this happens and you don't think it should have?

Check the formatting of your values to make sure they match. Also check that there aren't extra spaces in one of your inputs or lookup values.

8. What does the IFERROR function do? What do you need to be careful with if you use it?

Suppresses an error result and replaces it with a zero, a blank space, or text that you provide. It will suppress all error messages, even ones you may want to see.

9. What does the #NUM! error message generally indicate?

That there are numeric values in a function that are not valid. It also happens when the function is going to return a result that is too large or too small or can't find a solution.

10. What is a circular reference?

One that references itself. So if in Cell A1 I write =A1+B1 that is circular because to generate the answer in Cell A1 I would have to use the value in Cell A1. That would create a continuous loop if you actually tried to do it.

11. If you don't think you have a circular reference but Excel tells you you do, what should you check for?

That you haven't created an indirect circular reference. For example, if you write in Cell A1 =B1+C1 that looks fine. But if the value in C1 is calculated by =SUM(A:A) then you're using the value in Cell A1 to calculate the value in Cell C1 and can't also use it to calculate the value in Cell A1.

12. If you're trying to figure out what cells are feeding the value in a cell where can you go to do that?

Trace Precedents under Formula Auditing in the Formulas tab.

13. If Excel tells you you have too few arguments, what should you check for?

First, that you've included all required inputs for that particular function. In the function description anything listed with brackets is optional, but anything listed as text without brackets is not. Also, check that you have all of your parens and commas and quotation marks in the right places.

14. What can you do with a formula that just isn't working the way it should be?

Double-click on the formula and check that all of the

cell references are pointing to the right cells.

If you're copying a formula make sure that you used $ signs to lock any cell references that need to be locked.

Make sure that any options for that function were chosen properly. (Exact versus approximate, ascending vs. descending, etc.)

If you copied from Word into Excel make sure that you replace any curly quotes or smart quotes with straight quotes. Excel will not accept smart quotes.

CELL NOTATION

1. What is Cell A1 referencing?

The cell that's in Column A and Row 1.

2. Name two ways you can reference more than one cell in a function.

With a comma between individual cells, row references, or column references. Or with a colon to reference a range of cells, rows, or columns.

For example:

$$=SUM(A1, B1, C1)$$
$$\text{or} =SUM(A:A,B:B,C:C)$$
$$\text{or} =SUM(1:1,2:2,3:3)$$
$$\text{or} =SUM(A1:C1)$$
$$\text{or} =SUM(A:C)$$
$$\text{or} =SUM(1:3)$$

3. Can you reference a cell in another worksheet?

Yes. You just need to include the worksheet name reference as well.

4. Can you reference a cell in another workbook?

Yes. You just need to include the workbook name reference as well, but be careful doing so because the formula may not work if that other workbook is moved, renamed, or deleted.

5. What's an easy way to reference a cell in another worksheet or workbook?

Start your formula and then just click on the cell you need. Excel will write the cell reference for you.

BONUS: EXERCISES

Exercise 1

	A	B	C	D
1	**Customer Name**	**Units**	**Price**	**Product**
2	Albert Jones	5	$2.50	Widgets
3	Mark Smith	10	$5.00	Whatsits
4	Nancy Baker	5	$2.50	Whatsits
5	Albert Jones	10	$5.00	Whatsits
6	Mark Smith	5	$5.00	Whatsits
7	Nancy Baker	5	$5.00	Whatsits
8	Albert Jones	4	$5.00	Widgets
9	Mark Smith	3	$2.50	Widgets
10	Nancy Baker	2	$2.50	Widgets

Take the data table above and write formulas to calculate:

1. The total spent for each transaction.

2. The total number of units sold.

3. The total amount earned using SUMPRODUCT.

4. The average price per unit across the transactions.

5. Also build a grid from that data that has customer name in rows and product across the top and write formulas to calculate:

A. Amount spent per customer per product.

B. Number of units ordered per customer per product.

C. Average unit price paid per transaction per customer per product.

Exercise 2

Given the following numbers, write formulas to calculate the average, median, and mode as well as the mode.mult with room for four possible results.

$$10$$
$$10$$
$$10$$
$$20$$
$$50$$
$$300$$
$$300$$
$$300$$
$$40$$
$$50$$
$$1200$$
$$1200$$
$$1200$$
$$50$$

Exercise 3

Write a formula that takes the following data table and combines the values in each row to form a single entry with last name comma first name middle name with no additional spaces and the name in all caps.

(So, for example, change Amanda, Diane, and Cook from the first row into COOK, AMANDA DIANE in Cell D1.) Do this with one formula.

	A	B	C
1	**First Name**	**Middle Name**	**Last Name**
2	Amanda	Diane	Cook
3	Mark	David	Allen
4	Brad		Jones
5	Alejandro		Sanchez

Exercise 4

Build a simple discount table that gives customers $5 off if they spend $25 or more and $10 off if they spend $50 or more and then write a VLOOKUP function to find the discount for purchases of $5, $25, $45, $50, and $75. Then do the same with an IF or an IFS function.

Exercise 5

10
12
14
5
8
7
16
20
22
34

Given the above list of numbers, how would you write a formula to make the following calculations:

1. Looking from smallest value to largest value, what place in the order is 8?

2. Looking from largest value to smallest value, what place in the order is 22?

3. What value is the 6th smallest value?

4. What value is the 4th largest value?

5. How could you calculate a random whole number that is between the smallest value in this range and the largest value in this range using one formula to calculate the smallest and largest value as well as the random number?

Exercise 6

You have a project that you are managing. The start date of the project is July 1, 2019 and will need to be finished by August 30, 2019. Assume the only holiday is July 4, 2019.

1. Assuming a standard U.S. workweek with Saturdays and Sundays off, write a formula to calculate how many days you have to complete the project?

2. Assume that you have ten people assigned to this project and that you want to put them into two teams of five. Write a formula to calculate how many possible team configurations you have to choose from?

3. The project requires completing 500 widgets during the project period. Assuming that in the first three weeks you produce 68, 84, and 72 widgets, respectively, and that this phase of the project has six weeks for completion, and that there will be no significant changes to the production

rate, write a formula to determine if you will reach your goal.

Exercise 7

Take the following table of units sold by each of three sales people for each of three products.

	A	B	C	D
1		Jane	Javier	Mo
2	**Widgets**	25	22	24
3	**Whatchamacallits**	15	18	30
4	**Thingies**	12	20	15

1. Explain the formula and steps you would use to build a table that lists the salesperson name in rows and the product name in each column and remains linked to the original data table.

2. Write a formula that will look in the original table for the number of Whatchamacallits sold by Javier using a search for Javier's name.

3. Write a formula that will look in the original table for the number of Whatchamacallits sold by Javier assuming

that you won't know which column Javier is in nor will you know which column Whatchamacallits are in.

Exercise 8

1. Take the following value in Cell A1
$$\$121/hr$$

and write a formula that will extract the dollar portion of the entry only.

2. Write a formula to calculate at what point in the above entry the / starts?

3. You have a cube that is 2 foot by 2 foot by 2 foot. Write a formula to calculate the area of that cube.

4. Write a formula to calculate the area of the cube in meters.

Exercise 9

Explain how you would write a formula to calculate how often each of the following values occurs: 2, 2, 2, 6, 6, 6, 6, 8, 8, 9, 9, 9, 9

Exercise 10

You've been given a database that contains a thousand numbers in it and told to predict the most likely value. How would you approach this question?

BONUS: EXERCISE ANSWERS

Exercise 1 Answers

	A	B	C	D
1	**Customer Name**	**Units**	**Price**	**Product**
2	Albert Jones	5	$2.50	Widgets
3	Mark Smith	10	$5.00	Whatsits
4	Nancy Baker	5	$2.50	Whatsits
5	Albert Jones	10	$5.00	Whatsits
6	Mark Smith	5	$5.00	Whatsits
7	Nancy Baker	5	$5.00	Whatsits
8	Albert Jones	4	$5.00	Widgets
9	Mark Smith	3	$2.50	Widgets
10	Nancy Baker	2	$2.50	Widgets

Take the data table above and write formulas to calculate:

1. The total spent for each transaction.

Formula for Cell E2 is =B2*C2

This can be copied down to the rest of the rows in the table.

	A	B	C	D	E
1	**Customer Name**	**Units**	**Price**	**Product**	**Total Spent**
2	Albert Jones	5	$2.50	Widgets	$12.50
3	Mark Smith	10	$5.00	Whatsits	$50.00
4	Nancy Baker	5	$2.50	Whatsits	$12.50
5	Albert Jones	10	$5.00	Whatsits	$50.00
6	Mark Smith	5	$5.00	Whatsits	$25.00
7	Nancy Baker	5	$5.00	Whatsits	$25.00
8	Albert Jones	4	$5.00	Widgets	$20.00
9	Mark Smith	3	$2.50	Widgets	$7.50
10	Nancy Baker	2	$2.50	Widgets	$5.00
11	**Total**	**49**			**$207.50**

2. The total number of units sold.
=SUM(B2:B10)

This can also be created using the AutoSum option.

3. The total amount earned using **SUMPRODUCT**.
=SUMPRODUCT(B2:B10,C2:C10)

4. The average price per unit across the transactions.
=AVERAGE(C2:C10)

5. Also build a grid from that data that has customer name in rows and product across the top and write formulas to calculate:

See tables on next page for one possible way to arrange the grid of customer name and product for each question.

A. Amount spent per customer per product.

Assuming customer name is in Column H and product is in Row 1 in the Amount Spent table, in Cell I2 write the formula

=SUMIFS($E:$E,$A:$A,$H2,$D:D,I1)

and then copy it to the rest of the cells in the table.

Amount Spent		
	Whatsits	Widgets
Albert Jones	$ 50.00	$ 32.50
Mark Smith	$ 75.00	$ 7.50
Nancy Baker	$ 37.50	$ 5.00

Units Ordered		
	Whatsits	Widgets
Albert Jones	10	9
Mark Smith	15	3
Nancy Baker	10	2

Average Unit Price		
	Whatsits	Widgets
Albert Jones	$5.00	$3.75
Mark Smith	$5.00	$2.50
Nancy Baker	$3.75	$2.50

B. Number of units ordered per customer per product.

Assuming customer name is in Column H and product is in Row 6 in the Units Ordered table, in Cell I7 write the formula

=SUMIFS($B:$B,$A:$A,$H7,$D:D,I6)

and then copy it to the rest of the cells in the table.

C. Average unit price paid per transaction per customer per product.

Assuming customer name is in Column H and product is in Row 11 in the Average Unit Price table, in Cell I12 write the formula

=AVERAGEIFS($C:$C,$A:$A,$H12,$D:D,I11)

and then copy it to the rest of the cells in the table.

Exercise 2 Answers

Given the following numbers, write formulas to calculate the average, median, and mode as well as the mode.mult with room for four possible results.

10

10

10

20

50

300

300

300

40

50

1200

1200

1200

50

With the values in Cells A1 through A14:

To calculate the average use
=AVERAGE(A1:A14)

To calculate median use
=MEDIAN(A1:A14)

To calculate the mode use
=MODE.SNGL(A1:A14)

To calculate the multiple mode outcome, select four cells such as Cells D5 through D8 and then use
=MODE.MULT(A1:A14)

and finish with Ctrl + Shift + Enter rather than enter.

Exercise 3 Answers

Write a formula that takes the following data table and combines the values in each row to form a single entry with last name comma first name middle name with no additional spaces and the name in all caps.

(So, for example, change Amanda, Diane, and Cook from the first row into **COOK, AMANDA DIANE** in Cell D1.) Do this with one formula.

	A	B	C
1	**First Name**	**Middle Name**	**Last Name**
2	Amanda	Diane	Cook
3	Mark	David	Allen
4	Brad		Jones
5	Alejandro		Sanchez

You could use:

=UPPER(TEXTJOIN({", "," "},1,C2,A2,B2))

Or assuming Cells A7 and B7 contain the delimiters, you can use

=UPPER(TEXTJOIN(($A$7:$B$7),1,C2,A2,B2))

Or

=UPPER(TRIM(CONCATENATE(C2,", ",A2," ",B2)))

	A	B	C	D
1	First Name	Middle Name	Last Name	Last, First Middle
2	Amanda	Diane	Cook	COOK, AMANDA DIANE
3	Mark	David	Allen	ALLEN, MARK DAVID
4	Brad		Jones	JONES, BRAD
5	Alejandro		Sanchez	SANCHEZ, ALEJANDRO

Exercise 4 Answers

Build a simple discount table that gives customers $5 off if they spend $25 or more and $10 off if they spend $50 or more and then write a **VLOOKUP** function to find the discount for purchases of $5, $25, $45, $50, and $75. Do the same with an **IF** or **IFS** function.

	A	B	C	D
1	**Discount Table**			
2	**Purchase Amount**	**Discount**		
3	$0.00	$0.00		
4	$25.00	$5.00		
5	$50.00	$10.00		
6				
7	**Test Amounts**	**VLOOKUP**	**IF Function**	**IFS Function**
8	$5.00	$0.00	$0.00	$0.00
9	$25.00	$5.00	$5.00	$5.00
10	$45.00	$5.00	$5.00	$5.00
11	$50.00	$10.00	$10.00	$10.00
12	$75.00	$10.00	$10.00	$10.00
13				
14	**Row 8 Formulas**			
15	**VLOOKUP**	=VLOOKUP(A8,$A$3:$B$5,2)		
16	**IF Function**	=IF(A8<$A$4,$B$3,IF(A8<$A$5,$B$4,$B$5))		
17	**IFS Function**	=IFS(A8>=$A$5,$B$5,A8>=$A$4,$B$4,TRUE,$B$3)		

Above is one possible way to structure the problem. Using this table, in Row 8 for the VLOOKUP function you can then write the formula:

=VLOOKUP(A8,$A$3:$B$5,2)

Then in Row 8 for the IF and IFS functions you can write:

=IF(A8<$A$4,$B$3,IF(A8<$A$5,$B$4,$B$5))

Or

=IFS(A8>=$A$5,$B$5,A8>=$A$4,$B$4,TRUE,$B$3)

By using the dollar signs in the formulas this allows you to write the formula once and then copy it down to the remaining cells in that column.

Exercise 5 Answers

10
12
14
5
8
7
16
20
22
34

Given the above list of numbers, how would you write a formula to make the following calculations:

Formulas given below assume you entered the values in Cells A1 through A10, but the results should be the same no matter where you entered the values.

1. Looking from smallest value to largest value, what place in the order is 8?
    =RANK(8,A1:A10,1)
    The result should be 3.

2. Looking from largest value to smallest value, what place in the order is 22?
    =RANK(22,A1:A10)
    The result should be 2.

3. What value is the 6th smallest value?
    =SMALL(A1:A10,6)
    The result should be 14.

4. What value is the 4th largest value?
    =LARGE(A1:A10,4)
    The result should be 16.

5. How could you calculate a random whole number that is between the smallest value in this range and the largest value in this range using one formula to calculate the smallest and largest value as well as the random number?
    Using
        =RANDBETWEEN(SMALL(A1:A10,1),
                LARGE(A1:A10,1))

Exercise 6 Answers

You have a project that you are managing. The start date of the project is July 1, 2019 and will need to be finished by August 30, 2019. Assume the only holiday is July 4, 2019.

1. Assuming a standard U.S. workweek with Saturdays and Sundays off, write a formula to calculate how many days you have to complete the project?

> =NETWORKDAYS("July 1, 2019","August 30, 2019","July 4, 2019")

> =NETWORKDAYS.INTL("july 1, 2019", "august 30, 2019", ,"July 4, 2019")

2. Assume that you have ten people assigned to this project and that you want to put them into two teams of five. Write a formula to calculate how many

possible team configurations you have to choose
from?

$$=COMBIN(10,5)$$

**3. The project requires completing 500 widgets
during the project period. Assuming that in the first
three weeks you produce 68, 84, and 72 widgets,
respectively, and that this phase of the project has
six weeks for completion, and that there will be no
significant changes to the production rate, write a
formula to determine if you will reach your goal.**

This can be calculated using the FORECAST.LINEAR
function to predict output for weeks four, five, and six.

If you put the values for the first three weeks in Cells
A1 through B4 where Column A has the week number and
Column B has the number of widgets made in that week,
you can then use the following formulas to predict the
number of widgets that will be produced each week.

$$=FORECAST(4,\$B\$2{:}\$B\$4,\$A\$2{:}\$A\$4)$$
$$=FORECAST(5,\$B\$2{:}\$B\$4,\$A\$2{:}\$A\$4)$$
$$=FORECAST(6,\$B\$2{:}\$B\$4,\$A\$2{:}\$A\$4)$$

	A	B	C
1	Week	Widgets	
2	1	68	
3	2	84	
4	3	72	
5			
6			FORECAST
7	Week	Widgets	Formula
8	4	78.6667	=FORECAST(4,$B$2:$B$4,$A$2:$A$4)
9	5	80.6667	=FORECAST(5,$B$2:$B$4,$A$2:$A$4)
10	6	82.6667	=FORECAST(6,$B$2:$B$4,$A$2:$A$4)

Exercise 7 Answers

Take the following table of units sold by each of three sales people for each of three products.

	A	B	C	D
1		Jane	Javier	Mo
2	Widgets	25	22	24
3	Whatchamacallits	15	18	30
4	Thingies	12	20	15

1. Explain the formula and steps you would use to build a table that lists the salesperson name in rows and the product name in each column and remains linked to the original data table.

This can be done easily with the TRANSPOSE function. Highlight an area that is four cells by four cells, and type

=TRANSPOSE(A1:D4)

in the first cell while the others remain highlighted, and then use Ctrl+Shift+Enter to populate the four cells.

To remove the 0 value in the top left corner of the table you can go to the corresponding cell in the original table and type ="" into that cell and then hit Enter.

2. Write a formula that will look in the original table for the number of Whatchamacallits sold by Javier using a search for Javier's name.

=HLOOKUP("Javier",A1:D4,3)

3. Write a formula that will look in the original table for the number of Whatchamacallits sold by Javier assuming that you won't know which column Javier is in nor will you know which column Whatchamacallits are in:

=INDEX(A1:D4,MATCH("Whatchamacallits",A1:A4,0), MATCH("Javier",A1:D1,0))

Exercise 8 Answers

1. Take the following value in Cell A1, $121/hr, and write a formula that will extract the dollar portion of the entry only.
    =LEFT(A1,LEN(A1)-LEN("/hr"))

2. Write a formula to calculate at what point in the above entry the / starts?
    =SEARCH("/",A1)

3. You have a cube that is 2 foot by 2 foot by 2 foot. Write a formula to calculate the area of that cube.
    =2^3 or
    =POWER(2,3)

4. Write a formula to calculate the area of the cube in meters.
    =(CONVERT(2,"ft","m"))^3 or
    =CONVERT(POWER(2,3),"ft^3","m^3")

Exercise 9 Answers

Explain how you would write a formula to calculate how often each of the following values occurs: 2, 2, 2, 6, 6, 6, 6, 8, 8, 9, 9, 9, 9

Put the values into one cell each to make a table.

Copy those values to a new location and remove duplicates. (Or create your own table of the unique values.)

You now have two choices:

You can highlight the cells in the next column that are next to the unique values and use the FREQUENCY function to calculate occurrence of each one. This is an array function so be sure to use Ctrl+Shift+Enter instead of Enter.

Or, you could also solve the problem using the COUNTIF or COUNTIFS functions.

See the next page for an example of the original data placed into a table and then another table created to show just unique values.

For that table of unique values, the FREQUENCY formula is:

$$=FREQUENCY(A2:A14,C2:C5)$$

since the original values were in Cells A2 through A14 and the unique values were in Cells C2 through C5.

For the COUNTIFS function, the formula is,

$$=COUNTIFS(\$A\$2:\$A\$14,C2)$$

which is then copied down for each row in the table of unique values.

Either approach gives the result in Column D.

	A	B	C	D
1	**Entries**		**Value**	**Occurrence**
2	2		**2**	3
3	2		**6**	4
4	2		**8**	2
5	6		**9**	4
6	6			
7	6			
8	6			
9	8			
10	8			
11	9			
12	9			
13	9			
14	9			

Exercise 10 Answers

You've been given a database that contains a thousand numbers in it and told to predict the most likely value. How would you approach this question?

Start by graphing the results so that you can see whether the values are evenly distributed or skewed in some way.

Depending on the results of the graph you could then use the AVERAGE, MEDIAN, MODE.SNGL, or MODE.MULT functions to find the average value, median value, or the most frequently occurring value(s).

You could also create a frequency table using the FREQUENCY function if it looks like MODE.SNGL or MODE.MULT won't capture all of the top values.

ABOUT THE AUTHOR

M.L. Humphrey is a former stockbroker with a degree in Economics from Stanford and an MBA from Wharton who has spent close to twenty years as a regulator and consultant in the financial services industry.

You can reach M.L. at mlhumphreywriter@gmail.com or at mlhumphrey.com.

Made in the USA
Monee, IL
07 February 2022